CHARLES PEIRCE'S GUESS
AT THE RIDDLE

CHARLES PEIRCE'S GUESS at the RIDDLE

Grounds for Human Significance

John K. Sheriff

Indiana University Press
Bloomington and Indianapolis

The paper used in this publication meets the minimum
requirements of American National Standard for Information
Sciences—Permanence of Paper for Printed Library Materials,
ANSI Z39.48-1984.
Manufactured in the United States of America

Library of Congress Cataloging-in-Publication Data

Sheriff, John K., date
Charles Peirce's guess at the riddle : grounds for human
significance / John K. Sheriff.
p.   cm.
Includes bibliographical references and index.
ISBN 0-253-35204-5 (alk. paper). — ISBN
0-253-20880-7 (pbk. : alk. paper)
1. Peirce, Charles S. (Charles Sanders), 1839–1914.
I. Title.
B945.P44S47   1994
191—dc20
93-33835

1 2 3 4 5 99 98 97 96 95 94

For

my
family

CONTENTS

vii

Contents

FOREWORD

CHARLES SANDERS PEIRCE is now recognized the world over as a great philosopher in the classic sense, but his greatness is often attributed to his technical achievements and his speculative subtlety and breadth. Now John Sheriff gives us another Peirce: a visionary, a wise man, a seer. This is the Peirce who confronts the Sphinx portrayed in the opening quotation from Emerson, the Sphinx who from age to age persists in asking for the secret of the universe. For Peirce, the riddle addresses more than the enigmatic relation of mind and matter: it includes in its compass the purpose and meaning of human life. This was true also for Emerson, whose interest in the tale of the Sphinx was its human significance.

Peirce the scientific philosopher takes his turn at the riddle and delivers his guess: "three elements are active in the world, first, chance; second, law; and third, habit-taking." From this he builds in classic architectonic fashion—in the style of Aristotle, Kant, and Hegel—a bold and intricate system of thought, and for its heart he installs his now-famous general theory of signs. But, as Sheriff sees it, Peirce's success in explaining the universe and the interrelatedness of mind and matter yields to the rest of the Sphinx's riddle: *How then shall we live?* Sheriff's book gives Peirce's answer to this vital question.

This is a book about human meaning—not in the technical and analytical sense, but as an answer to the human predicament. Sheriff writes for those whose interest in Peirce is rooted in the humanities: in theology, semiotics, literary theory, and esthetics. He expounds Peirce's original

unified theory of the universe—from cosmogony to semiotics—and develops Peirce's message for human life: there is
no need for resignation or for despair, for there is a real "possibility of unlimited intellectual and moral growth and *of*
unlimited survival for the human community." Sheriff's
work is a defense of Peirce's philosophical sentimentalism
and a compelling recommendation to modern thinkers to
reconsider Peirce's cosmology. Sheriff follows Peirce's argument for the primacy of sentiment, and he concludes that
Peirce has given us a theory *we can live with*. The tone is
religious in the best sense.

Sheriff's book makes an important contribution to the
philosophy of life and to the humanities in general. The
Peirce that Sheriff reveals gives us a positive integrative alternative to popular pessimistic and relativistic approaches to
life and meaning. Once again, civilization appears to be on
the brink of catastrophe, or at least a regress to darker times,
and it is urgent that we begin to build a secular philosophy
of life that incorporates the positive features of religion. I
believe that Peirce's philosophical sentimentalism as ex-
pounded by Sheriff may be what is called for—at least it
makes a promising beginning. Sheriff is neither insistent nor
aggressive; he merely invites us to accept Peirce's theory as a
working hypothesis and consider the benefits.

Sheriff is not the first to apprehend the revolutionary
import of Peirce's philosophy for the humanities—for the
philosophy of life. In his 1989 Jefferson Lecture, Walker
Percy argued that with his theory of signs Peirce had laid the
groundwork for a much-needed coherent science of man,
but that this Peircean unified *and unifying* theory remained to
be worked out. Yet, if it is so revolutionary and so important, why has it lain fallow for so long? I believe mainly for
two reasons. First, because Peirce's vision is a view from a
high and somewhat perilous philosophical peak, a complex
architectonic cosmology that has always presented a formi-

dable front. But Sheriff has taken up Percy's challenge and has succeeded in extracting from Peirce's complex system of thought a manageable and attractive essence. Whether Sheriff has extracted a pure essence is an interesting question that will no doubt be much debated, although, for Sheriff's purpose, what counts is more the spirit of Peirce than the letter of his thought.

The second impediment to the serious consideration and sustained study of Peirce's philosophy of life has been Peirce himself—his own unattractive and largely failed life. How can his philosophy of life be worth much if it could not serve to better guide its own author? But Peirce's gift is not a practical guide to successful living: it is a general philosophy of human progress, a natural philosophy that integrates human life with the universe as a whole, and the emphasis is on community. The accidents of an individual life should not detract from the lesson of the general philosophy that the particular existence fails to exemplify. As Bertrand Russell enjoyed pointing out, what Jesus taught is not well exhibited in his angry destruction of the fig tree that had failed to bear fruit out of season or in his furious expulsion of the money changers from the Temple of Jerusalem; yet we do not for those examples spurn his philosophy of love.

The Peirce scholar should be aware that this is not a technical study of Peirce, although there is a fine summary explication of Peirce's philosophy and there are some interpretive moves that will interest and stimulate the most serious scholar. While this book may, on the technical side, call for a somewhat relaxed approach, in a different sense it calls for the most intense and compelling thought—that musing and creative current, that wisdom that can tap into Peirce's visionary genius and his elegantly retold guess at the great riddle of worthwhile existence.

Nathan Houser

PREFACE

This relation between the mind and matter . . . is the problem which has exercised the wonder and the study of every fine genius since the world began; from the era of the Egyptians and the Brahmins, to that of Pythagoras, of Plato, of Bacon, of Leibnitz, of Swedenborg. There sits the Sphinx at the roadside, and from age to age, as each prophet comes by, he tries his fortune at reading her riddle.
—Ralph Waldo Emerson, "Nature"

THE HUMAN PREDICAMENT, the situation of human intelligence, the conditions of our use of signs as Charles S. Peirce perceived them are as follows: truth is in the future, but in our consciousness we cannot help but assent to what we perceive to be the case in the particular contexts and language games within which we live. Likewise, at every moment that we perceive beauty and goodness we experience no doubt about what beauty and goodness are.

One of the assumptions underlying much current literary theory is that there are levels of sign use that correspond to kinds of people or to degrees of linguistic sophistication. For example, there are those naive persons who in their *everyday use of language* are blind to the re-presentational nature of language and for whom signs seem to be signs of natural facts. Such persons are only aware of these apparent facts (living, nature, objectivity, laws), and they carry on what is sometimes referred to as classical discourse.

Then, purportedly, there is a second group of people or level of language use. The second level is *use of language to show life*. Here we have the artists who "recontextualize"[1] *everyday use of language* to serve their expression (creation, showing forth) that fictionalizes ordinary life (actions, objects, sayings), thereby making *everyday use of language* consciously symbolic. We often think of this use of language as indirect, because the language games of ordinary life are used indirectly as fable, parable, irony, poetry, drama, satire, etc. In general, this use of language makes us conscious of our perception of the world.

The third level is of course that used by philosophers of language, literary critics, linguists, etc. They *use language to analyze living and showing*, that is, they analyze the language used by levels one and two. Moreover, they analyze their own use of language in analyzing the use of language. These are the sophisticates, the modernists and poststructuralists. The implicit goal of much recent linguistic, literary, and cultural theoretical studies is to get the whole world to level three discourse, as if that would allow us to start all over without the blindness that seems to be inherent in sign use. We would usher in the millennium by getting everyone to be meta-metalinguists (discourse theorists).

Of course, we know better. Levels one and two are not levels we graduate from as stages in our linguistic maturity; the three kinds of language uses do not correspond to kinds of people or to classical, modern, and poststructural epistemes. Nor is there an ontological continuum here. In Peirce's triadic sign theory *every sign* embodies all three levels of use. In *every* sign is a triadic relation of sign-object-interpretant. Level one sign use is the space platform I just left behind *and* the ship in which I travel but cannot see (signs functioning as representamens in triadic relations). When I jump to the porthole to look back, I see only level two, the supreme fiction that I take to be a mimesis of the fundamental realities (signs functioning as objects in triadic relations), and what I say/think about what I see is always level three (signs functioning as interpretants in triadic relations). Levels one, two, and three use/consciousness of language are not habits one can break.

Such, according to Peirce, is the human predicament. Peirce forces us to come to terms with what King Oedipus learned a long time ago but what many scientists and even more humanists today seem never to grasp—that ours is a human perspective, not sometimes, but always. We are like Achilles and Tortoise in the fable Douglas Hofstadter tells in *Gödel, Escher, Bach: An Eternal Golden Braid*.[2] They have some "pushing-potion" that when drunk pushes them into a print of M. C. Escher, and if there is a print within that print they can drink again and be pushed into it, and so on. They also have some "popping-tonic" that allows them to pop out of the print they have pushed into and should allow them to pop back into reality. One problem Achilles and Tortoise have is that the world of every print feels as real as the reality from which they started. After pushing into a few of Escher's prints successively, they begin popping out only to find that they have no way of knowing when they are back into the real world.

If that fable dramatizes the 'situatedness' of humans in a universe of signs, how then shall we live?

This question may seem to be a shift in modes of discourse because it introduces a subjective, ethical concern into what was formerly an objective discussion of the human predicament. It switches from science to the humanities. However, this question only makes explicit what is implicit in most seemingly objective discussions of human discourse and theory. Regardless of what theories one accepts about limits of human knowledge, the political nature of human discourse, or the conventionality or relativity of values, any intelligent, social being asks this ethical question with seriousness. In fact, I suspect every work on language/discourse/literary theory is to some extent asking and answering the question, How should we act?

If the human predicament is as we have described it

above, and if we do ask the question, What then? the philosophy of Charles Sanders Peirce is of great importance to us because it gives us a theory of cosmic and human meaning that does not lead to the dead-end nothingness of pure form or to the decentering and deconstruction of the human subject, but to the possibility of unlimited intellectual and moral growth and *of unlimited survival* for the human community.

Charles Peirce, whose architectonic theory of cosmos, mind, signs, logical thought, and ultimate goodness is finally becoming widely known and appreciated, believed that feeling and thought, esthetics and reason are mutually interdependent. Peirce's answer to the question, How shall we live? is found in his analysis of the possibility of controlled conduct by an intelligence capable of learning from experience. The credibility of this answer derives partially from its being a part of Peirce's unified theory of all that is.

Stephen W. Hawking, professor of mathematics at Cambridge University, was quoted as follows in an article entitled "A Unified Theory of the Universe Would Be the Ultimate Triumph of Human Reason":

> [I]f we do discover a complete theory, it should in time be understandable in broad principle by everyone, not just a few scientists. Then we shall all, philosophers, scientists, and just ordinary people, be able to take part in the discussion of the question of why it is that we and the universe exist. If we find the answer to that, it would be the ultimate triumph of human reason—for then we would know the mind of God.[3]

However he may ultimately be judged, Charles Sanders Peirce aimed at such a unified theory. He asked the same age-old questions Hawking asks: "What is the nature of the universe? What is our place in it and where did it come from? Why is it the way it is? How or why were the laws and the initial state of the universe chosen?" And Peirce spent a lifetime working out some answers.

Peirce's unified theory and its implications for human behavior is the subject of this book. I have endeavored to describe what Peirce discovered and/or created, and approved, before he died: a coherent, cosmological/logical/moral system that we might as well call a unified, comprehensive, general theory of everything. It was the triumph of his life, yet a triumph coupled with the painful awareness that he was not going to get the book or books written and published that would spell out the theory to which he had devoted a lifetime of intellectual effort.

Even though many fine studies have illuminated various themes in Peirce's thought, and though most Peirce scholars now affirm the "essential unity, the architectonic, even organic quality"[4] of Peirce's philosophy, no overview of Peirce's comprehensive theory from a humanist (humanities) perspective has heretofore been available. It is clear in manuscripts Peirce left incomplete and unpublished that he had hoped to provide such a work himself.

As early as 1886 Peirce was making outlines and writing manuscript for a book that would outline his comprehensive theory. One of the drafts of this proposed book is headed "Notes for a Book, to be entitled 'A Guess at the Riddle,' with a Vignette of the Sphynx below the Title." Peirce's remark after this caption shows what he thought the significance of his work to be: "And this book, if ever written, as it soon will be if I am in a situation to do it, will be one of the births of time."[5]

As the following chapters will show, Peirce understood the question of the sphinx to be not only about the relation of mind and matter (as Emerson envisioned the question in the quotation at the head of the Preface), but also of the purpose and meaning of human life.[6] It may seem ironical to those who know Peirce primarily as scientist, mathematician, and logician that the importance of Peirce's theory is being increasingly discovered in the humanities, as evidenced by a burgeoning of Peirce scholarship in theology, semiotics, literary theory, and esthetics. It is primarily for this audience, persons who have become acquainted with Peirce through scholarship in these fields, for whom this work is written.

Because the goal of this work is to provide a brief account of Peirce's comprehensive system as a context for human meaning, I will necessarily give a summary treatment of many concepts that are worthy of more attention and in many cases have been treated in book-length studies. The major contributions of this work will be (1) to provide an overview of Peirce's unified system, explaining the hypothetical commonality of physical, psychical, and semiotic phenomena, and (2) to show what his theory implies about the significance of human consciousness and behavior. The work offers a holistic conception of Peirce's theory that can serve as an adequate and accurate context for those who wish to discover the implications of Peirce's thought for humanistic questions. The chapter titles suggest the range of interests and disciplines for which this work provides the larger context of Peirce's unified theory.

I am deeply aware of the extreme complexity of the philosophic task that Peirce conceived, and I do not want to leave the impression with readers that Peirce left us a clearly conceived and concisely expressed unified theory that we can understand by reading a few writings selected from his works. That is definitely not the case. One of the works Peirce proposed for himself in 1893, "The Principles of Philosophy: or Logic, Physics, and Psychics, considered as a unity, in the Light of the Nineteenth Century," was to be twelve volumes in length. Although this and other proposed works were never entirely completed, Peirce left drafts, sometimes multiple drafts, of parts of them. Edward C.

Moore suggested in the preface to the first volume of *Writings of Charles S. Peirce: A Chronological Edition* that it would take approximately 104 five-hundred-page volumes to publish Peirce's complete works.[7] The unfinished nature of Peirce's work and the sheer volume of it pose difficulties for all seeking to understand or propagate Peirce's ideas. That is why works such as this one are sorely needed.

Peirce said in a draft for "A Guess at the Riddle" (c. 1887)[8] that "To erect a philosophical edifice that shall outlast the vicissitudes of time, my care must be, not so much to set each brick with nicest accuracy, as to lay the foundations deep and massive" (1.1). The following chapters do not attempt to evaluate every concept in Peirce's philosophy, but to show how Peirce's analyses of esthetics, ethics, logic, and all human consciousness and cognition rest on the foundations of and are situated in Peirce's grand philosophical edifice, his architectonic theory of cosmos, mind, and signs.

Peirce has argued convincingly that theories/paradigms/generals shape the future, mold reactions to themselves, and mediate the meaning of life for us: this is their nature and significance. Therefore, Peirce's unified theory of the universe, offering a world context for human consciousness and enabling meaningful identity and action, is potentially a powerful, positive force in culture. This potential is one motivation for writing this synthesis of Peirce's great intellectual achievement—a unified theory of the universe and of mind that gives cosmic significance to human behavior.

Rather than begin by defining Peirce's basic categories and concepts in the abstract, I have chosen to describe the world according to Peirce, thereby letting the theory and the world this perspective opens up evolve together for the reader. This approach has several advantages.

First, it avoids needless repetition.

Second, Peirce maintained throughout his life that the

dyadic sign and dualistic thinking that see everything as external, autonomous, isolated objects are remnants of classical Western thinking that is very limiting. In 1887 he looked forward to the time "when the palpable falsity of that mechanical philosophy of the universe which dominates the modern world shall be recognized" (6.553). He found little basis for "the common belief that every single fact in the universe is precisely determined by law" (6.36) and asserted that any evolutionary account of the universe must account for the evolution of laws. Placing Peirce's cosmology at the beginning effectively separates Peirce from commonly held notions that he rejected and helps the reader to make the paradigm shift Peirce's triadic theory requires. Even though some think Peirce's "Cosmogonic Philosophy" (his theory of the creation and evolution of the universe) to be among the most puzzling and difficult parts of his thought, it helps to clarify why Peirce's general theory of signs based on a triadic sign and triadic relations does not separate language and reality, does not perceive language as an autonomous, purely formal system independent of mind and matter, does not perceive reality as an autonomous, ontological system independent of mind and language. Peirce's account of the evolution of the universe allows us to *see* what these statements mean.

Moreover, it seems reasonable to begin a book seeking to explicate the humanistic dimension of Peirce's thought with cosmology because that is consistent with Peirce's own experience. He said, "I came to the study of philosophy not for its teaching about God, Freedom, and Immortality, but intensely curious about Cosmology and Psychology" (4.2). Also he said that "Metaphysics has to account for the whole universe of being. It has, therefore, to do something like supposing a state of things in which that universe did not exist, and consider how it could have arisen" (6.214).

Preface

Finally, by letting Peirce's theory emerge from his description of his perception of the world, we are constantly aware that what we have is a phenomenological perspective, a human view. Such an approach does not prejudge implicitly or explicitly the accuracy of Peirce's theory. Peirce's invitation, and the invitation of this book, is to consider hypothetically what would be the case if his theory were correct.

I hope this approach allows the work to have a narrative quality and allows readers to experience often the joy of discovery as they are carried along by the thought of an original philosopher whose intellect was so developed it still waits to be fully understood.

Any introduction to Peirce's theory is inevitably challenging for many reasons, not the least of which are the originality of his thought and the strangeness of his terminology. My advice to readers unfamiliar with Peirce's thought is to read this book rapidly the first time, especially the first three chapters. One's grasp of Peirce's triadic thinking emerges and becomes more and more clear as the many faces of his general theory appear in successive chapters.

ACKNOWLEDGMENTS

WHILE THIS WORK was in progress, I drew material from the Preface, chapter 1, and chapter 2 for a short paper entitled "A Preface to Peirce's Guess at the Riddle," which was presented at the 1992 meeting of the Semiotic Society of America and will appear in *Semiotics 1992*, the proceedings of the seventeenth annual meeting of the SSA. Some of the material in chapter 5 appeared earlier in a review article in *Semiotica: Journal of the International Association for Semiotic Studies* entitled "Legitimating Purposive Action" (Jan./Feb. 1993, pp. 155–71). Finally, parts of chapter 3 are from my treatment of signs in *The Fate of Meaning: Charles Peirce, Structuralism, and Literature* (Princeton, N.J.: Princeton University Press, 1989).

I am indebted to Jørgen Dines Johansen, Vincent Colapietro, Eugene Kaelin, Michael Raposa, Mark Bandas, Robert Corrington, and the late David Savan for their encouragement and the critique they have given to my work on Peirce. I am especially grateful to Nathan Houser for his critical reading of this manuscript. Of course, these persons are not responsible for or necessarily in agreement with the ideas put forth in this study.

CHARLES PEIRCE'S GUESS
AT THE RIDDLE

PEIRCE'S COSMOGONIC PHILOSOPHY

[T]he problem of how genuine triadic relationships first arose in the world is a better, because more definite, formulation of the problem of how life first came about . . . (6.322)

Peirce was familiar with the biblical account of creation, with cosmological theories from the time of Democritus to his own day, and with the evolutionary theories of Charles Darwin, Chevalier de Lamarck, and Clarence King. Peirce's cosmogony was indebted to these theories, yet he did not fully agree with any of them. He rejected a mechanical, necessitarian conception of the universe that "leads abruptly up to hard, ultimate, inexplicable immutable law on the one hand, and to inexplicable specification and diversification on the other" (6.63). And he rejected any evolutionary theory that was not thoroughgoing, that arbitrarily separated matter and law, that excluded time and logic from the evolutionary process.

Peirce believed that metaphysics should account for the whole universe of being, physical and psychical. Consequently, he said, "to proceed in a logical and scientific manner, we must, in order to account for the whole universe, suppose an initial condition in which the whole universe was non-existent, and therefore a state of absolute nothing" (6.215).

I

Peirce anticipated two objections to this method of proceeding. He acknowledged that we cannot even think "before the beginning" without getting tangled up in our words if we take them literally. "For time is itself an organized something, having its law or regularity; so that time itself is a part of the universe whose origin is to be considered. We have therefore to suppose a state of things before time was organized" (6.214). From inside time, being, existence, language, human existence, a fixed place—in short, from inside the symbol system that is intelligence—we try to conceive of the initial condition before the universe existed, before the beginning (because before time), before being, before existent things, before symbols, before thinking, before logic, before facts, before actuality. Therefore, in trying to conceive of the initial condition before the universe existed and to consider how it could have arisen, "we do not mean in speaking of the first stages of creation before time was organized, to use 'before,' 'after,' 'arising' and such words in the temporal sense" (6.214). At any point in the infinitely remote past or future one would already be *in time* (time is continuous) and would find already in irreducible triadic relation:

Firstness, Secondness, Thirdness;
possibility, fact, law;
quality, reaction, symbol (representation);
feeling, effort, habit.

The reader need not understand the triadic relation of these phenomena yet, since our first goal is to show Peirce's effort to account hypothetically, by abstractive observation, for how time and triadic relations might have come into being.

The other obstacle he anticipated was that this theorizing might be confused with religious belief. Peirce considered religious beliefs to be practical in that we act upon them. He asked readers only to adopt his cosmological account provisionally, as a scientist adopts a hypothesis to test by investigation. In retrospect we see that Peirce's theory based on three categories and triadic relations conforms without any resistance to the Hebrew-Christian theory of a world created and controlled by a triune God.[1] It would of course be perfectly consistent with Peirce's critical common-sensism[2] to take seriously an account handed down through millennia from the old Babylonian philosophers. Peirce frequently drew the parallel between his theory and the Genesis account but warned that the figurative language of the Genesis account is even more vague than his own. If in an expression like "mind of God" one imagines brains and ganglia like our own and an aged man, the analogy is more misleading than helpful (6.199). Having said that Peirce's cosmogony conforms without resistance to the biblical story of creation, it is not a contradiction to say that his cosmology is a thoroughgoing evolutionary theory.

From Nothing . . . Something

Since Peirce aimed at a metaphysics that accounts for everything, he must begin with nothing and explain how something comes from nothing. As we begin to trace his theory of origins, perhaps Peirce's reflections on his theory in 1909, five years before his death, will clarify what Peirce tried to accomplish and the limits of his success.

> [T]he problem of how genuine triadic relationships first arose in the world is a better, because more definite, formulation of the problem of how life first came about; and no explanation has ever been offered except that of pure chance, which we must suspect to be no explanation, owing to the suspicion that pure chance[3] may itself be a vital phenomenon. In that case, life in the physiological sense would be due to life in the metaphysical sense. Of course, the fact that a given individual has been persuaded

of the truth of a proposition is the very slenderest possible argument for its truth; nevertheless, the fact that I, a person of the strongest possible physicistic prejudices, should, as a result of forty years of questionings, have been brought to the deep conviction that there is some essentially and irreducibly other element in the universe than pure dynamism may have sufficient interest to excuse my devoting a single sentence to its expression. (6.322)

From this statement it can be anticipated that Peirce's theory will account for the origin of triadic relations, the role of chance, and the "vital" metaphysical element in his theory.[4] To summarize that account is the goal of this chapter. The importance of the following account of creation for subsequent chapters is the description of the three categories of being and the triadic relations fundamental to Peirce's thought.

The nothing from which something must have come in the infinitely remote initial state was "pure zero," indeterminacy. That is, it was not the nothing of negation.

> For *not* means *other than*, and *other* is merely a synonym of the ordinal numeral *second*. As such it implies a first; which the present pure zero is prior to every first. The nothing of negation is the nothing of death, which comes *second* to, or after, everything. But this pure zero is the nothing of not having been born. There is no individual thing, no compulsion, outward or inward, no law. It is the germinal nothing, in which the whole universe is involved or foreshadowed. As such, it is absolutely undefined and unlimited possibility—boundless possibility.
>
> So of *potential* being there was in that initial state no lack. (6.217)

"Potential," in Peirce's usage, means indeterminate yet capable of determination in any specific case (6.185–86).

Some readers may be helped to equate this "germinal

nothing" that was before the beginning with God in the Christian myth—the absent God who is outside our realm of experience and beyond our capacity to understand, but the source of all existent things and all beauty and order.[5]

Qualities/Monads: Firstness

Although nothing *necessarily*, that is, according to the deductive logic of reason, resulted from the Nothing of boundless freedom, something did.

> The logic of freedom, or potentiality, is that it shall annul itself . . . unbounded potentiality became potentiality of this or that sort—that is, of some *quality*. . . . Thus the zero of bare possibility, by evolutionary logic, leapt into the *unit* of some quality. (6.219–20)

> Out of the womb of indeterminacy we must say that there would have come something, by the principle of Firstness, which we may call a flash. (1.412)

This "evolutionary logic," leap, "principle of Firstness," "flash," may be thought of, Peirce said, as "hypothetic inference." The logic of evolution is from the vague to the definite, from the indefinite future to the irrevocable past, from undifferentiated to the differentiated, from the homogeneous to heterogeneity (6.191). We may imagine a series of contractions moving from the vague to the definite, the abstract to the particular. We can imagine the evolutionary logic to have been:

> Something is possible,
> Red is something;
> [Therefore] Red is possible. (6.219)

Thus, the vague potentiality of everything in general and nothing in particular became definite and contracted into qualities, which "are mere eternal possibilities" (6.200). If qualities sprang "into a preliminary stage of being by their own inherent firstness" (6.199), "[t]he very first and most fundamental element we have to assume is a Freedom, or Chance, or Spontaneity, by virtue of which the general vague nothing-in-particular-ness that preceded the chaos took a thousand definite qualities" (6.200).

The first active element in the world, then, was chance or freedom that gave rise to qualities.[6] These qualities were sentient, sense-qualities. The consciousness of quality is not a "*waking* consciousness—but still, something of the nature of consciousness. A *sleeping* consciousness, perhaps" (6.221). The fact that it is "sleeping" or "slumbering" does not make it less intense, "For it is the absence of *reaction*—of feeling another—that constitutes slumber, not the absence of the immediate feeling that is all that it is in its own imme-diacy" (6.198). Peirce named this consciousness "*quale-consciousness*" (6.221–37). Possibility, quality, potential consciousness, and feeling are synonymous and all have *quale*-consciousness.

> The *quale*-consciousness is not confined to simple sen-sations. There is a peculiar *quale* to *purple*, though it be only a mixture of red and blue. There is a distinctive *quale* to every combination of sensations so far as it is really synthesized—a distinctive *quale* to every work of art—a distinctive *quale* to this moment as it is to me—a distinc-tive *quale* to every day and every week—a peculiar *quale* to my whole consciousness. (6.223)

Each *quale* is all that it is in and for itself without reference to any other. Many qualities may blend (but not without losing their individual identities) and become a unity, one element, one quality, a sui generis *quale*-consciousness, entirely sim-ple. Metaphorically, quality or *quale*-consciousness is "soli-tary and celibate" (6.234). Our own "consciousness, so far as it is contained in an instant of time, is an example of *quale*-consciousness" (6.231).

The nature of quality to have a *unity, quale*-consciousness, is the metaphysical element in Peirce's view of the universe. All unities (e.g., Kant's synthetic unities, the unity of logical consistency, the unity of the individual object, specific unity) "originate, not in the operations of the intellect, but in the *quale*-consciousness upon which the intellect operates" (6.225). The kind of consciousness that originates in intellect Peirce called vividness, liveliness, or concentration, but he argued that "no *unity* can *originate* in concentration" (6.227). "The unity of consciousness is . . . not of physiological origin. It can only be metaphysical" (6.228).

Reactions/Dyads: Secondness

Now let us return to our creation story, before time began. So far we have said (1) that "nullity consists in the possibility of the monad" (1.453), (2) that qualities, by their own inherent Firstness (freedom, chance), sprang up from the "general vague nothing-in-particular-ness" of "unbounded potentiality," and (3) that already in this preliminary stage of being was what we might most clearly refer to as potential consciousness, a feeling independent of any action, reaction, or reflection, a metaphysical *unity*. Even though this primal chaos had no regularity or physical aspect, "there was an intensity of consciousness there, in comparison with which all that we ever feel is but as the struggling of a molecule or two to throw off a little of the force of law to an endless and innumerable diversity of chance utterly unlimited" (6.265).[7]

The qualities did not spring up in isolation, Peirce said, but "in reaction upon one another, and thus into a kind of existence" (6.199). Peirce did not object to those who wished to describe the springing up of qualities as "God determining so and so," or to those who described the reaction or existence of qualities as the "mind of God" (6.199). At one point he referred to the original potentiality as "the Aristotelian matter or indeterminacy from which the universe is formed" (6.206). In his own scheme of things, he had simply moved from Nothing to chaos. The units of quality, the *quale*-elements, while their inward nature is unity, as a multitude are a Babel, a bedlam, a chaos of fortuitously wandering units. If nothing prevents one from springing to this kind of existence, nothing will prevent a million. If each is what it is irrespective of anything else, there will be no regularity, only endless multiplicity and variety (6.237).

Continuity/Triads: Thirdness

In Peirce's thought, "real existence . . . consists in regularities" (6.265). Therefore this original chaos where there was no regularity "was in effect a state of mere indeterminacy, in which nothing existed or really happened" (1.411). In this chaos, unpersonalized feeling "sporting [a word borrowed from Darwin, meaning chance variations of fecundity] here and there in pure arbitrariness, would have started the germ of the generalizing tendency. Its other sportings would be evanescent, but this [generalizing tendency] would have a growing virtue. Thus, the tendency to habit would be started; and from this . . . all the regularities of the universe would be evolved" (6.33).

The stage is now set for the next leaps or flashes of evolution that set creation in process, a process that continues today and will continue into the infinite future. Just as nullity, absolute indetermination, consists of the possibility of determining monads of quality, units consist of the possibility of dyads of reaction, and brute reactions consist of the possibility of continuity. Peirce, acknowledging the

Hegelian influence, said that "the possibility evolves the actuality" (1.453).

The Tendency to Take Habits—
The Key to It All

Chance or spontaneity made room for this tendency to habit, the generalizing tendency, which made possible the creation of all that is. The absolute individual has no regularity and of course cannot be realized in sense or thought. From the moment that anything has regularities (hence duration), there are dyadic reactions of force and triadic relations of generalization and continuity. Chance (unbounded freedom and spontaneity) and continuity (generality) were inherent in the original, general potentiality. Chance works toward diversity; continuity, toward uniformity. Chance has the character of feeling; continuity, of habit-taking. Chance evolves qualities and reactions; continuity evolves laws of action, *is*, in fact, the general law of action.[8]

This, in a nutshell, is Peirce's explanation of conformity to law. "[S]ince law in general cannot be explained by any law in particular, the explanation must consist in showing how law is developed out of pure chance, irregularity, and indeterminacy" (1.407).

We should now at least be able to understand Peirce's hypothesis that "all laws are results of evolution; that underlying all other laws [all regularities of nature and of mind] is the only tendency which can grow by its own virtue, the tendency of all things to take habits" (6.101). With great elaboration, of which I will give only samples, Peirce demonstrated that the tendency to habit can account for "the main features of the universe as we know it—the characters of time, space, matter, force, gravitation, electricity, etc" (6.34)—and for the phenomena of feeling, growth, and growing complexity that appear in the universe and for which a mechanistic philosophy cannot account. Peirce was convinced to the end of his life that he had found the key to unlock the mysteries of cosmology and psychology (the mysteries that had attracted him to philosophy in the first place), and he never ceased using it: "[I]t is clear that nothing but a principle of habit, itself due to the growth by habit of an infinitesimal chance tendency toward habit-taking, is the only bridge that can span the chasm between the chance medley of chaos and the cosmos of order and law" (6.262).

Perhaps the clearest example in Peirce's account of how hypothetically time and triadic relations might have come into being is Peirce's use of a clean blackboard as a diagram of the original vast potentiality. In giving this example Peirce took the role of a teacher in front of his classroom explaining his theory. The extensive quotations that follow are interesting not only for the ideas but for the image of Peirce they portray.

Granted, Peirce began, the blackboard is a continuum of two dimensions and that for which it stands is a continuum of an indefinite multitude of dimensions; the board is a continuum of possible points, that for which it stands a continuum of possible dimensions of quality. At first there are no points on the board and no dimensions in the original potentiality.

> I draw a chalk line on the board. This discontinuity is one of those brute acts by which alone the original vagueness makes a step toward definiteness. There is a certain amount of continuity in this line. Where did this continuity come from? It is nothing but the original continuity of the blackboard which makes everything upon it continuous. (6.203)

If there is any discontinuity on the board, it can only be produced "by the reaction between two continuous surfaces into which it is separated, the white surface and the black surface" (6.203).

> The whiteness is a Firstness—a springing up of something new. But the boundary between the black and white is neither black or white, nor neither, nor both. It is the pairedness of the two. It is for the white the active Secondness of the black; for the black the active Secondness of the white. . . .
>
> We see the original generality like the ovum of the universe segmented by this mark. However, the mark is a mere accident, and as such may be erased. It will not interfere with another mark drawn in quite another way. There need be no consistency between the two. But no further progress beyond this can be made, until a mark will *stay* for a little while; that is, until some beginning of *habit* has been established by virtue of which the accident acquires some incipient staying quality, some tendency toward consistency.
>
> This habit is a generalizing tendency, and as such a generalization, and as such a general, and as such a continuum or continuity. . . .
>
> The whiteness or blackness, the Firstness, is essentially indifferent as to continuity. It lends itself readily to generalization but is not itself general. [It is quality, possibility, monadic, Firstness.] The limit between the whiteness and blackness is essentially discontinuous, or antigeneral. It is insistently *this here*. [It is reaction, specific fact, dyadic relation, Secondness.] The original potentiality is essentially continuous, or general.
>
> Once the line will stay a little after it is marked, another line may be drawn beside it. Very soon our eye persuades us there is a *new* line, the envelope of those others [e.g.,].[9] [The new line is law, general fact, triadic relation, Thirdness.] This rather prettily illustrates the logical process which we may suppose takes place in things, in which the generalizing tendency builds up new habits from chance occurrences. The new curve, al-

though it is new in its distinctive character, yet derives its continuity from the continuity of the blackboard itself. . . .

Many such reacting systems may spring up in the original continuum; and each of these may itself act as a first line from which a larger system may be built, in which it in turn will merge its individuality. (6.203–207)

Peirce, in his thoroughgoing way, imagines the Platonic world of ideas as well as the existing world to be evolved in this way. In fact there may be many such Platonic worlds, out of one of which "is differentiated the particular actual universe of existence in which we happen to be" (6.208). However, he describes the same process when he shows that his generalizing tendency accounts for time, space, matter, force, gravitation, electricity as we know them.

Consider, for example, his account of the hypothetical origin of time. Since time is a regularity, it is a product of evolution. It was probably not uniform or continuous in its flow in the germinal stage since in the original chaos the habits and the tendency to take them might have been weak and of short duration. There may have been several flows or streams of time before their generalizing tendencies of qualities reacting with each other would have been strengthened and become "bound into something like a continuous flow" (1.412).

So one stream might branch into two, or two might coalesce. But the further result of habit would inevitably be to separate utterly those that were long separated, and to make those which presented frequent common points coalesce into perfect union. Those that were completely separated would be so many different worlds which would know nothing of one another; so that the effect would be just what we actually observe. (1.412)

Spatial extension and substances would have developed as pairs react to create facts, develop habits of reacting with other pairs ("which will constitute a spatial continuum"), and develop bundles of habits ("which will be substances") (1.413, 414).

I will draw these illustrations to a close after one more example. This paragraph might be called Peirce's short account of Newtonian symmetry. Habits, Peirce said, consist in the permanence of some relation; "each law of nature would consist in some permanence, such as the permanence of mass, momentum, and energy" (1.415).

> The substances carrying their habits with them in their motions through space will tend to render the different parts of space alike. Thus, the dimensionality of space will tend gradually to uniformity; and multiple connections, except at infinity, where substances never go, will be obliterated. At the outset, the connections of space were probably different for one substance and part of a substance from what they were for another; that is to say, points adjacent or near one another for the motion of one body would not be so for another; and this may possibly have contributed to break substances into little pieces or atoms. But the mutual actions of bodies would have tended to reduce their habits to uniformity in this respect; and besides there must have arisen conflicts between the habits of bodies and the habits of parts of space, which would never have ceased till they were brought into conformity. (1.416)

Peirce does not typically leave broad generalizations unsupported. For example, he develops an extensive molecular explanation of habit, studies the habits of protoplasm, and always accounts for the law of habit *and* "its peculiar characteristic of not acting with exactitude" (6.260).

Theoretically, then, in the infinite past before anything

existed there were no uniformities (which amounts to a tau-
tology since "real existence" for Peirce is regularity). In the
infinite future there should come a time when there is no
indeterminacy or chance, but complete reign of law. "But at
any assignable time in the past, however early, there was already some tendency toward uniformity; and at any assignable date in the future there will be some slight aberrancy
from law" (1.409). All things, from atoms to people, have
the tendency to form habits, "a greater probability of acting
as on a former like occasion than otherwise" (1.409), and all
retain an element of chance or freedom. It is the essential
nature of the tendency to take habits to grow.

> [The tendency to take habits] is a generalizing tendency;
> it causes actions in the future to follow some generaliza-
> tion of past actions; and this tendency is itself something
> capable of similar generalizations; and thus, it is self-gen-
> erative. We have therefore only to suppose the smallest
> spoor of it in the past, and that germ would have been
> bound to develop into a mighty and over-ruling principle,
> until it supersedes itself by strengthening habits into ab-
> solute laws regulating the action of all things in every re-
> spect in the indefinite future. (1.409)

This is the hypothetical process that accounts for the
three kinds of phenomena, three modes of being, that Peirce
finds in the universe. Peirce names these Firstness, Secondness, and Thirdness. The categories of his architectonic are
merely the definition of these three kinds of phenomena,
and his general theory of signs is an attempt to describe their
interrelationships.[10] In logic they are beginning, end, and
process. In biology they are arbitrary sporting, heredity, and
the process whereby the accidental characteristics become
fixed, that is, chance, law, and the tendency to take habits.
In our experience, in psychology we might say, Firstness,
Secondness, and Thirdness are feelings, reaction-sensations,

and thought. The following are other names for, or rather manifestations of, the same triads:

qualities, real existent things, representation
feeling, reaction (change of feeling), habit
monads, dyadic relations, triadic relations
possibility, fact, law.
God, Jesus, Holy Spirit

But we cannot fully appreciate Thirdness, the triadic relation of these phenomena, until we understand the close connection of nature and mind, of law and thought. Since the tendency to take habits is the one fundamental law of evolution, "is the sole fundamental law of mind, it follows that the physical evolution works towards ends in the same way that mental action works towards ends . . . " (6.101g). The regularities of mind as well as those of nature must be regarded as the products of growth. The original chaos was like a confused dream in which nothing really existed. As things "are getting more and more regular, more persistent, they are getting less dreamy and more real" (1.175). In fact, as we shall see in the next chapter, Peirce regards matter as mind whose habits have become so fixed that it loses the powers of forming and losing them. Thus matter is partially deadened mind (6.101–102). In the hypothetically infinitely remote future when "the world becomes an absolutely perfect, rational, symmetrical system," there would be no element of pure chance, no chance deviations from law, no habit-taking. Mind would be crystallized, dead (6.33). Feeling, growth, habit-taking (i.e., life) exists only where there is chance (freedom, spontaneity). "Wherever chance-spontaneity is found, there in the same proportion feeling exists. In fact, chance is but the outward aspect of that which within itself is feeling" (6.265).

From the boundless potentiality of nothing, from God if you wish, springs variety, continuity, reality *and* the feeling of unity, the metaphysical sense of life. Peirce's answer to the question, "What is God's present function?" was "Creation."

> I am inclined to think (though I admit that there is no necessity of taking that view) that the process of creation has been going on for an infinite time in the past, and further, during *all* past time, and, further, that past time had no definite beginning, yet came about by a process which in a generalized sense, of which we cannot *easily* get much idea, was a development. I believe Time to be a reality, and not the figment which Kant's nominalism proposes to explain it as being. . . . I think we must regard Creative Activity as an inseparable attribute of God. (6.506)

However we express it, chance/God is the vital element in the universe that gave rise to the tendency to habit that accounts for all order and laws of nature and mind. Therefore, the creation of the universe and the development of reason "is going on today and will never be done" (1.615). "To believe in a god at all," Peirce queried, "is not that to believe that man's reason is allied to the originating principle of the universe?" (2.24). Peirce's theory of that alliance is the subject of the next chapter.

2

MIND

The creation of the universe, which did not take place during a certain busy week, in the year 4004 B.C., but is going on today and will never be done, is [the] very creation of Reason. (1.615)

In spite of all the work being done in linguistics, psychology, and biology, mental phenomena are still today very mysterious, and there is no general theory of mind that explains them satisfactorily. Therefore, the extensive theory of mind Peirce arrived at nearly a hundred years ago is particularly interesting. In this chapter we will take the first step in explaining his theory of mind. That is, we will show how mental phenomena (feeling, consciousness, ideas, thought) fit into Peirce's evolutionary cosmology and that they are no different in kind from other phenomena in the universe. In Peirce's theory, mental phenomena incorporate the same three modes of being and follow the same evolutionary law as do physical phenomena.

Peirce charged psychologists with having failed to distinguish between mind and consciousness (not to be equated with self-consciousness, which we will treat later). They fail, Peirce said, to make clear what a psychical phenomenon is or to establish a theory of mind "which can compare for an instant in distinctness to the dynamical conception of matter" (7.364). Peirce sets out to remedy these shortcomings or at least to offer hypotheses and suggestions for scientifically testing hypotheses. In keeping with our practice

17

throughout this book, our goal is not to give Peirce's critique of psychology as it existed at the time of his writing (1902 in the case of the above critique), but to present Peirce's theory without further comparison.

Mental Phenomena

In the previous chapter we discussed the hypothetical origin of Firstness, Secondness, and Thirdness as three modes of being and tried to show that the evolution of these modes of being and the evolution of the universe as physical entity are one and the same thing. But the evolution of the physical universe is only half of the story. The tendency of all things to take habits, "the only tendency that can grow by its own virtue" (6.101) underlies *all* other laws. "[T]his same tendency is the one sole fundamental law of mind" (6.101). Peirce's hypothesis is that "chance must give birth to an evolutionary cosmology in which all the regularities of nature *and of mind* are regarded as products of growth" (6.102, italics added). It would be mistaken, Peirce said, to "conceive of the psychical and the physical aspect of matter as two aspects absolutely distinct" (6.268).

> Viewing a thing from the outside, considering its relations of action and reaction with other things, it appears as matter. Viewing it from the inside, looking at its immediate character as feeling, it appears as consciousness. These two views are combined when we remember that mechanical laws are nothing but acquired habits, like all the regularities of mind, including the tendency to take habits, itself; and that this action of habit is nothing but generalization, and generalization is nothing but the spreading of feelings. (6.268)

Theoretically, the law of continuity, the continuous spread of feeling, born of chance, can produce general ideas, "mental" associations if you will. Thirdness, then, which we have been referring to as "habit-taking" and "continuity" might just as well be called "mind," "intelligence," or "reason." In fact, Peirce uses the terms interchangeably. "A reason," he says, "has its being in bringing other things into connexion with each other; its essence is to compose: it is triadic, and it alone has a real power" (6.343).

Reason, as Peirce uses it here, is not merely the human faculty, which does embody some measure of reason. Rather, it is the habit-taking, continuity, generalization that has the mode of being that Peirce calls Thirdness. "The very being of the General, of Reason, *consists* in its governing individual events" (1.615). This being its essence, it can never be fully perfected but "must always be in a state of incipiency, of growth" (1.615). It would have no being if it did not have something to work upon. This is true of all Thirdness. Hence, "Reason requires as a part of it the occurrence of more individual events than ever can occur. It requires, too, all the coloring of all qualities of feeling" (1.615). The development of Reason, then, consists "in embodiment, that is, in manifestation" (1.615). This is why Peirce described mind as external, consciousness as inward; mind is essentially Thirdness, consciousness is essentially Firstness. Thirdness is no "thing" but the "power" or "process" that brings Firstness and Secondness into the regularity of relation that is "reality." There was no order or regularity until there was Thirdness—until the habit-taking tendency developed (according to Peirce's evolutionary cosmogony) or until God spoke (Genesis). Or as Joseph Esposito puts it in *Evolutionary Metaphysics*, "The 'first condition' (MS. 1105) of creation must . . . be expression." "Expression" here means "consciousness-of in the form of a conception or feeling."[1] The perpetual task of reason/Thirdness/expression is creation, the embodiment and manifestation of Firstness, Secondness, and, yes, Thirdness.

Charles Peirce's Guess at the Riddle

The law of the continuous spreading of feeling (of generalization), Peirce said, "will produce a mental association; and this I suppose is an abridged statement of the way the universe has been evolved" (6.143). Peirce expects to be asked after making such a statement whether a blind force can bring ideas together.

> I point out that it would not remain blind. There being a continuous connection between the ideas, they would infallibly become associated in a living, feeling, and perceiving general idea. . . . No, I think we can only hold that wherever ideas come together they tend to weld into general ideas; and wherever they are generally connected, general ideas govern the connection; and these general ideas are living feelings spread out. (6.143)

General ideas, Peirce said, "are just as much, or rather far more, living realities than the feelings themselves out of which they are concreted" (6.152). In mental phenomena instantaneous feelings/qualities flow together to form general ideas/regularities which influence and are influenced by each other. This is merely a repeat of what we said about physical phenomena in chapter 1. The expression "a universe of ideas" is an apt description of the cosmos. It is a very coherent set of general ideas.

Since we tend to associate living, feeling, and perceiving with persons and mind, we may be tempted to ask, In whose mind is this set of ideas? And we might say that the universe is the mind of God or God's idea. In fact Peirce, upon being questioned about God and religion, argued that the universe is "a great symbol of God's purpose," "precisely an argument," "a great poem," "a symphony," and is comparable to "a painting" (5.119). My only objection to this way of thinking is that it causes us to attribute consciousness to God instead of to ideas. If God is conscious, Peirce would say, it is because he *is*, not has, consciousness.

Or to put it another way, if God has consciousness he is *in* creation; he is part or all of creation.[2]

Given the fact that mechanical laws and the regularities of mind are nothing but acquired habits, and that the action of habit is nothing but generalization, and generalizations nothing but the spread of feeling, we would expect that a general idea has the same "unified living feeling" a person does (6.270). Or, more accurately, a person is a general idea.

We have difficulty attributing consciousness (we are still speaking of feeling, not self-consciousness) to entities such as ideas, on the one hand, or protoplasm on the other. Maybe if we look more fully at the reasons Peirce attributes some degree of consciousness to all reality, the notion will seem more like a serious scientific hypothesis and less like something out of a tale by Edgar Allen Poe.

First let's consider once more what an idea is. We have said that it is something general. Generality and continuity are the same. Time, the universal form of change, can serve for us as an example of something general and continuous. As a general, every unit of time is made up of a continuum of lesser units that differ from the unit they together make up. It may be a decade, a year, a month, a day, an hour, a minute, a second, and so on infinitely, toward smaller or larger units. Since time has the mode of being of Thirdness, continuity, it "cannot exist unless there is something to undergo change and to undergo a change continuous in time there must be a continuity of changeable qualities" (6.132). Thus, "Time logically supposes a continuous range of intensity of feeling" (6.132). Any finite interval of time is always divisible and therefore contains an innumerable series of feelings. "When these become welded together in association [continuity, unity, generalization, expression], the result is a general idea" (6.137). The intrinsic quality of an idea is feeling. Just as every quality is monadic (that is, has a *unity*) regardless of how many qualities might merge to

compose it, every idea has a feeling, *quale*-consciousness.
And just as all feelings will "spread continuously" and "affect certain others which stand to them in a peculiar relation
of affectability" (6.104), ideas will affect other ideas. And
just as every quality loses its identity when it merges with
other qualities to form a new quality, ideas lose intensity as
they spread but "gain generality and become welded with
other ideas" (6.104). Thus, every idea, every regularity in
the universe (such as time) has varying degrees of Firstness,
Secondness, and Thirdness, i.e., quality, relations, continuity; monadic, dyadic, triadic relations.

If we would rewrite the above paragraph replacing
"idea" with "person," the paragraph would be just as accurate. Peirce on several occasions compared ideas and persons
and always found that ideas have all the attributes and functions of human consciousness. Even when he compared a
person and a word he found little or no difference, except in
intensity of feeling. His unshakable conclusion was that a
person is a general idea and that all matter is made of qualities whose relations have various degrees of stability.[3]

At one hypothetical extreme, before the beginning, was
pure chance, chaos, feeling; at the other hypothetical extreme of the continuum is pure uniformity, absence of feeling. In between, in time, in the process of evolution, are all
the phenomena of the universe. In such phenomena as gravitation or solid masses "evolution has so nearly approached
its ultimate limit, that nothing even simulating irregularity
can be found in it" (7.515). But in the human mind, "the
most plastic of all things," and in the organic world, the
world of protoplasm, "we find plasticity and evolution still
at work" (7.515). The mind, Peirce said, is "a chemical
genus of extreme complexity and instability," and matter
may be regarded as "mind whose habits have become fixed
so as to lose the powers of forming and losing them"
(6.101). Feeling-consciousness, the one metaphysical ele-

ment in Peirce's cosmology, exists in proportion to the degree to which chance-spontaneity is found.

It was as a result of studying naked protoplasm under
various conditions and stimuli that Peirce concluded that
mind seems to have a continuous extension in space as well
as in time. Just as feeling and consciousness "in one instant
directly influences, or spreads over into, the succeeding instant . . . the feeling at any point in space appears to spread
and to assimilate to its own quality, though with reduced
intensity, the feelings in the closely surrounded places"
(6.277). That feelings should affect other feelings close to
them is in keeping with his principle of continuity and perhaps will help us grasp Peirce's notion that every general
idea/person has a similar "unified living feeling" or consciousness. "All that is necessary . . . to the existence of a
person is that the feelings out of which he or she is con-
structed should be in close enough connection to influence
one another" (6.270). The generalization of feeling should
of course spread to include all within a person to create a
"unified living feeling," but it should also spread even beyond, though "further generalization will have a less lively
character" (6.271). Peirce ponders the question of whether it
would be possible to subject to a scientific test the idea that
there is such a thing as a corporate personality made up of
the generalized feeling of several personalities. If such a
thing is possible, Peirce said, "*Esprit de corps*, national sentiment, sym-pathy, are no mere metaphors" (6.271). To be of
one mind and spirit seems to be the inherent goal, the evolutionary tendency of reason.

For Peirce to say that a person is a general idea and that
the description of how ideas evolve is a description of how
the universe evolved does not make him a nominalist, which
is the last thing Peirce would want to be called. But he does
insist that nature and idea are manifestations of the same law.
The ability to feel, reproduce (to spread, merge, and form

new feeling and ideas), and to take habits are attributes of protoplasm and ideas. On the other hand, it would be equally wrong to assume that because feeling, consciousness, and reason are the products of evolution that Peirce is a materialist believing in some kind of Laplacean or Spencerian deterministic philosophy. "Instead of supposing mind to be governed by blind mechanical law, [Peirce's evolutionary theory] supposes the one original law to be the recognized law of mind, the law of association, of which the laws of matter are regarded as mere special results" (6.277). Both mind and matter are "mere" results of the one original law, the tendency to take habits. And it is because feelings of quality are the Firstness without which there could have been no regularity (Secondness) or continuity (Thirdness) that Peirce "attributes to all matter a certain excessively low degree of feeling together with a certain power of taking habits" (6.277).[4]

To say, then, that mental phenomena are governed by law is not to say that they are describable by a formula like $E = mc^2$. Rather, it is to say that "there is a living idea, a conscious continuum of feeling, which pervades them, and to which they are docile" (6.152). In mental phenomena, as in physical phenomena, instantaneous feelings/qualities flow together to form general ideas/regularities that influence and are influenced by each other.

Consciousness and Self-Consciousness

So far we have tried to show that, according to Peirce's theory, mental phenomena evolved from the universal tendency of all things toward generalization, that general ideas are the generalization of feelings. Since the intrinsic quality of a general idea is feeling, it is capable of further generalization and in so doing brings other ideas along with it (6.135).

If we understood fully the nature of ideas, which are

feelings of consciousness when viewed from within and signs when viewed from without, and how ideas interact with and control each other, we would have a complete understanding of the universe and of logical thought. That is why, as we shall see later, Peirce's general theory of signs is a general theory of everything in the universe.

So far we have tried to look at consciousness objectively, as cosmic phenomena. This approach emphasizes the point that consciousness/feeling is not only something that is within us; we are within it. We do not have it; it has, or is, us. Having established that consciousness is the unified living feeling of a general idea and that a person may be thought of as a general idea, we may now shift our focus and consider the consciousness of a person.

Peirce draws a sharp distinction between mind and consciousness. Consciousness in itself is nothing but feeling; mind is the continuity of consciousness. Again it is important to emphasize that "feeling," which Peirce equates with consciousness, is the "immediate element of experience, generalized to its utmost" (i.e., Firstness) (7.365), and not feelings as objects of thought (which like all generals involve Firstness, Secondness, and Thirdness). As we have seen in the account of Peirce's evolutionary cosmology, a measure of feeling is everywhere to the degree that chance operates, but "feeling in any ascertainable degree is a mere property of protoplasm, perhaps only of nerve matter" (7.364). Since biological organisms exhibit the phenomena of mind, it is not surprising, Peirce said, that mind and feeling are confused. But "feeling is nothing but the inward aspect of things, while mind on the contrary is essentially an external phenomenon" (7.364).

The analogy Peirce gives to illustrate the external nature of mind is the relation of electric current to the wire it passes along. It used to be thought that electric current moved through the electric wire. This is an error analogous to thinking that mental powers are located or reside in various locations in the brain. Scientists have determined, for example, where in the brain the powers of speech are located by demonstrating that if you cut out a piece of the brain the subject is deprived of the ability to speak. We now know that an electrical current is wholly external to a wire and that "in" the wire is the only place from which it is cut off. Would anyone now accept the interruption of the electric current caused by snipping the wire as proof that electricity travels in the wire? If you cut out a lobe of the brain you certainly put an end to speaking. Peirce says that to have his inkstand filched would have the same effect; he would be unable to continue his discussion until he got another. The inkstand, the brain, and we might add the tongue, "have the same general relations to the functions of the mind" (7.366). It is more true, Peirce says, "that the thoughts of a living writer are in any printed copy of his book than that they are in his brain" (7.364).

Another example of how mind is an "external" phenomenon is our knowledge of language. When we say we know English, we do not mean that we have all the words and rules of the English language in our minds, or even one English word in mind. But if we think of an object, an English word will come to mind. If we think of two things relating, English nouns and verbs in a certain sequence will come to mind. And so on.

Mind is not synonymous with consciousness, and it has not been understood, Peirce said, because mental phenomena have not been subjected to the same resolute scientific investigation that material events have. Such investigation has been prevented by the delusion that mind is just consciousness.

Having shown that mind and consciousness are distinct and simultaneously interdependent, we can turn to self-consciousness, to the particular perspective of a *conscious person*, which will in turn lead us to Peirce's treatment of logical thought.

First, what is self-consciousness, and how does it fit into Peirce's theory? How much of consciousness can we be conscious of? What is the nature of human cognition? What do we consciously experience? The answers to all these questions are implicit in the very nature of the three phenomena in the Peircean universe.

Let us review the three modes of being that emerged from the hypothetical evolutionary process described in chapter 1 and that, according to Peirce, make up all creation, including the human mind and consciousness. As these appear *in consciousness* they are:

> first, feeling, the consciousness which can be included with an instant of time, passive consciousness of quality, without recognition or analysis; second, consciousness of an interruption into the field of consciousness, sense of resistance, of an external fact, or another something; third, synthetic consciousness, binding time together, sense of learning, thought. (1.377)

For a person, feelings, then, comprise immediate consciousness:

> that kind of consciousness which involves no analysis, comparison or any other process whatsoever [i.e., Thirdness], nor consists in whole or in part of any act by which one stretch of consciousness is distinguished from another [i.e., Secondness], which has its own positive quality which consists in nothing else, and which is of itself all that it is, however it may have been brought about. (1.306)

But the Firstness of consciousness, the instantaneous consciousness, immediate consciousness, as a thing-in-itself, is like every other First in the Peircean universe, purely hypothetical. The only consciousness that can be known is generalized, has duration, relates to a process. Immediate feelings, then, can only be contemplated in memory that "is an articulated complex and worked-over product which differs infinitely and immeasurably from feeling" (1.379). The experience of Firstness, the only Firstness that we can be conscious that we are conscious of, is always Third-Firstness: ideas, thoughts, signs of Firstness.

Just as immediate feeling is the consciousness of Firstness, a sense of polarity or reaction is the consciousness of Secondness. Peirce's examples are helpful here:[5]

> Besides Feelings, we have Sensations of reaction; as when a person blindfold suddenly runs against a post, when we make a muscular effort, or when any feeling gives way to a new feeling. (6.19)

> While I am seated calmly in the dark, the lights are suddenly turned on, and at that instant I am conscious, not of a process of change [which would be Thirdness], but yet of something more than can be contained in an instant. I have a sense . . . of there being two sides to that instant. A consciousness of polarity would be a tolerably good phrase to describe what occurs. (1.380)

We experience sensations when we are acted upon by something out of our control. Such an event has to happen in a particular moment, can happen only once, and is therefore antirational, antigeneral. "Remembering a sensation," Peirce said, "is not at all the same thing as having it" (7.543). As with Firstness, "remembering" a sensation is as close as we get to a sensation *in conscious thought*.

The consciousness of a process of change negated in the earlier quotation is the consciousness of Thirdness:

> This is the kind of consciousness which cannot be immediate, because it covers a time, and that not merely because it continues through every instant of that time, but

because it cannot be contracted into an instant. It differs from immediate consciousness, as a melody does from one prolonged note. Neither can the consciousness of the two sides of an instant, or a sudden occurrence, in its individual reality, possibly embrace the consciousness of a process. This is the consciousness that binds life together. It is the consciousness of synthesis. (1.381)

Therefore, Peirce said, when you ask what is in your mind at any moment, you cannot begin to tell the whole truth or to even know. Because of the indefinite continuity of consciousness,

What is present to the mind during the whole of an interval of time is something generally consisting of what there was in common in what was present to the mind during the parts of that interval. And this may be the same with what is present to the mind during any interval of time. . . . If a succession of thoughts have anything in common this may belong to every part of these thoughts however minute, and therefore it may be said to be present at every instant. This element of consciousness which belongs to a whole only so far as it belongs to its parts is termed the matter of thought. (7.352)

Another reason we cannot know or say all that is in our mind is that

consciousness [as feeling] must reach a considerable vividness before the least reflex feeling of it is produced. That it is really felt is shown by the fact that a greater effort of attention would detect it. There is as it were, an upper layer of consciousness to which reflex consciousness, or self consciousness is attached. A moderate effort of attention for a second or two only brings a few items in to the upper layer. But all the time the attention lasts, thousands of other ideas, at different depths of consciousness, so to speak, that is literally, of different degrees of vividness, are moving upwards. These may influence our other thoughts long before they reach the upper layer of reflex consciousness. There are such vast numbers of ideas in consciousness of low degrees of vividness that I think it may be true that our whole past experience is continually in our consciousness, though most of it sunk to a great depth of dimness. I think of consciousness as a bottomless lake, whose waters seem transparent, yet into which we can clearly see but a little way. (7.547)

Self-consciousness (which Peirce equated with attention, concentration, and reflex consciousness) is limited to the general, to what is common to a series of ideas in the mind, and to these according to a particular process of how ideas relate to each other. Feeling is independent of self-consciousness except as a generalized memory. Sensations of reactions are not part of self-consciousness, but our reflex feeling "that *there is* a feeling" (7.547) is a consciousness of some external force acting upon us. A sense of a reaction between the self and another separates the self and the not-self. Self-consciousness, then, requires that something represent something else. It requires signs, which is the same as to say it requires signs of signs. In short, it requires thought. All consciousness of which we are conscious has the character of Thirdness.

3

SIGNS

[T]here are three elements of cognition: thoughts, the habitual connection between thoughts, and processes establishing a habitual connection between thoughts. (7.355)

In the foregoing account of Peirce's evolutionary cosmology, which hypothetically begins with nothing and arrives at thought, a subtle transition occurs somewhere along the way. We started describing Firstness (feeling of quality, chance, particularity) and ended by saying all thought is Thirdness (rule controlled, generality). The transition was from an emphasis on ontology to an emphasis on phenomenology, from an exterior, hypothetically objective view of the developing cosmos to a view from within. Since the fundamental law of mind is the same as the fundamental law of the universe, there is never a clear break or division between the ontological and phenomenological. Yet to the degree that one of these views is dominant, the other is absent or hypothetical.

Even though we can never fully separate physical and psychical reality in Peirce's theory, evolution hypothetically moves from Firstness to Secondness to Thirdness (there could be no Secondness without Firstness and no Thirdness without Firstness and Secondness), but human perception is almost exclusively of the nature of Thirdness. Thus, what is first in the order of creation or evolution is Firstness, oneness, the monad, chaos; what is first in human experience is

Charles Peirce's Guess at the Riddle

Thirdness, triadic relation, representation, continuity. This, of course, is why all treatment of anything outside of Thirdness is purely hypothetical. Or to put it in Peircean terms, our only experience or perception of Firstness or Secondness is always for us Third-Firstness or Third-Secondness (this point will be further clarified later in this chapter). What is last in the order of evolution is first in human experience. Thought is representation; it is *signs of signs*.

Just as there is almost no chance/feeling left in such evolutionary habits as gravity, there is almost nothing ontological left in signs of signs. Our only experience of Firstness or Secondness is mediated by Thirdness.[1] That is, we experience only *signs* (which are already triadic relations) of Firstness, Secondness, and Thirdness. And in our thought we experience only signs of signs, mediation, pure form. However, that does not mean that we are separated from any*thing*. Our perspective is very much an inside view. Ours is the point of view of a living consciousness, of an idea in a universe of ideas. This consciousness is not an abstract nothing, an idly spinning wheel that does no work. It is part of the creative force in the universe, the only real creative power.

If seen within this context, Peirce's theory of signs is not just a matter of interest to linguists and logicians. It is part of his cosmology and his account of ongoing creation, which implicitly or explicitly answers such questions as, What is the place of humans in the universe? How is logical thought possible? What is reality? What is truth? What is good? It is the comprehensiveness of Peirce's theory, explaining the evolution of both physical and psychical phenomena, that makes it so intriguing. Before we proceed to give Peirce's answers to the above questions that have always been asked by consciousnesses capable of reason, let's first explain how Peirce accounts for the ability of a mind to reason, to learn from experience.

For a mind to have the power of investigation, to be able to pass from doubt to belief, to be capable of logical criticism, it must, Peirce said, have its ideas follow one after another in time, and it must be aware that one idea is determined by another that was previously in the mind (7.346). What follows then is not a comprehensive account of Peirce's sign theory, but a demonstration of how, according to Peirce's theory, ideas follow other ideas in time and how one idea is determined by another that was previously in the mind.

We have already established in our treatment of consciousness in the previous chapter that nothing is present to the mind in any one instant except a *quale*-consciousness (6.231), which is gone before we can think, "This is present to me" (5.289). The most finite thought covers a time and is at no instant present. Neither is the succession of ideas that makes reason possible present to the mind. Like the experience of a whole day or year, a succession of ideas "is something which can be lived through; but not be present in any instant; therefore, which can not be present to the mind at all" (7.348). It follows that there is nothing in the mind in the present instant that is of intellectual significance for what it is in itself. Every cognition has value "as standing for some object to which it relates" (7.355). From the moment that there is thought everything is a sign. And these signs are capable of forming new ideas and new habits of relating in the mind in a manner analogous to the way elements of Firstness, Secondness, and Thirdness form ideas and regularities in the cosmos.

If we look at the character of a sign, its *triadic* and *generative* nature, we will understand how one idea follows another in time.[2]

In Baldwin's *Dictionary of Philosophy and Psychology* (1902) Peirce defined a sign as "Anything which determines something else (its *interpretant*) to refer to an object to which itself refers (its *object*) in the same way, the interpretant becoming in turn a sign, and so on *ad infinitum*" (2.303). And in his unpublished "Syllabus," written about the same time as the above article, Peirce stated:

> A *Sign*, or *Representamen*, is a First which stands in such a genuine triadic relation to a Second, called its *Object*, as to be capable of determining a Third, called its *Interpretant*, to assume the same triadic relation to its Object in which it stands itself to the same Object. The triadic relation is *genuine*, that is its three members are bound together by it in a way that does not consist in any complexus of dyadic relations. . . . The Third . . . must have a second triadic relation in which the Representamen, or rather the relation thereof to its Object, shall be its own (the Third's) Object, and must be capable of determining a Third to this relation. All this must equally be true of the Third's Third and so on endlessly. (2.274)

The triadic relation described in the first definition of a sign quoted above may be visualized thus:

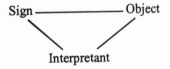

In the second statement quoted above, Peirce inserts First, Second, and Third. To avoid confusion it is important to emphasize immediately that because signs are just that, signs-of what they represent, they have a formal *and* ontological character. (I will develop this further in subsequent pages.) Consequently, sign theory must deal with formal as well as ontological categories of Firstness, Secondness, and

Thirdness. Peirce is saying here that every triadic thought-sign has some qualities in itself that distinguish it (it is a representamen); it is connected in some way with the thing it signifies (its object); and it is interpreted to thought as another sign (an interpretant).

Consequently, a sign functioning as a representamen (which Peirce calls a sign in the *sign*-object-interpretant relation), whether it is a thought or feeling, is a First to the degree that it is immediately present. A representamen can be no more than an "absolutely simple and unanalyzable" feeling, "a mere sensation without parts," "simply an ultimate, inexplicable fact" (5.289). "Whenever we think," Peirce says, "we have present to the consciousness some feeling, image, conception or other representation, which serves as a sign . . . *to* some thought which interprets it" (5.283). The "thought which interprets it," the interpretant, must be able to cause a second triadic connection in which the relation-of-the-sign-to-its-object in the first triad becomes the object of the interpretant (which assumes the position of a sign, i.e., representamen, in the new triad). Again it may be helpful to visualize the process of how an interpretant of a sign in a sign-object-interpretant relation becomes a sign in a new triadic relation, and so on.

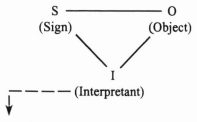

The relation-of-the-sign-to-its-object in the first triad becomes the object of the interpretant, which assumes the position of a sign in a new triad.

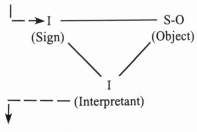

"And so on endlessly."

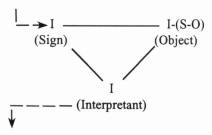

"[A]nd this, and more, is involved in the familiar idea of a Sign; and as the term Representamen is here used, nothing more is implied" (2.274).

If we analyze this simple diagram, we will begin to see that the unlimited complexity of the objects of thought and the generative nature of signs *make it possible for a consciousness to become aware of its own processes.* First of all, Peirce's definition of "object" is very encompassing:

> The Objects—for a sign may have any number of them—may each be a single known existing thing or thing believed formerly to have existed or expected to exist, or a collection of such things, or a known quality or relation or fact, which single Object may be a collection, or whole of parts, or it may have some other mode of being, such as some act permitted whose being does not prevent its negation from being equally permitted, or something of a general nature desired, required, or in-

variably found under certain general circumstances. (2.232)

Any sign or collection of signs that a person has experienced in the past can become an object in the representamen-object-interpretant relationship that allows signs to be represented, i.e., to have meaning, to be thought about.

Secondly, the above graphics show that there is an element of causation running through our consciousness, which will be more easily understood when we treat the "percipuum" in the next chapter. Here we need only to say that the causation by which the thought in any one moment determines the next thought is of the nature of reproduction, and therefore a part of every thought continues in the succeeding thoughts. Every sign is interpreted by a subsequent sign or thought in which the-relation-of-the-sign-to-its-object becomes the object of the new sign. Not only does a sign refer to a subsequent thought-sign that interprets it, it also stands *for* some object through a previous thought-sign. The only way a sign can stand for any object, regardless of how complex or artificial, is by referring to it through previous thought. Since we are conscious only of previous thoughts and the most finite thought covers a time, immediate consciousness of thought-signs is not possible. The thought present in the mind is meaningful only by virtue of its relation to subsequent interpretant-thoughts that give us information about their objects reflectively. Meaning, then, "lies not in what is actually thought [immediately present], but in what this thought may be connected with in representation by subsequent thoughts; so that the meaning of a thought is altogether something virtual" (5.289). Meaning exists only as the dynamic relation of signs. To the degree that life has meaning, it is a train of thought.

We can imagine, Peirce said, a mind that reasons but

never knows that it reasons. Such a mind would not be aware that its conclusion was a conclusion or was derived from anything before it; such a mind would have no conception of a right or wrong method of thinking and would be incapable of criticizing its own operations (7.346).

For the mind to have its ideas follow after one another in time *and* to be aware that one idea is determined by another that was previously in the mind, it is not only necessary that one idea should produce another, but it is also necessary that *a mental process* should produce an idea. For logical thought to be possible, for a mind to be able to criticize its own operations, a process must be present to the mind. And this process must consist of absolutely distinct parts existing at different times. When one part is in the mind, the others are not. To unite them we must suppose a consciousness running through the time. In other words, a process must be able to produce an idea if the logical mind is to be aware of the process:

> So that of the succession of ideas which occur in a second of time, there is but one consciousness, and of the succession of ideas which occur in a minute of time there is but one consciousness, and so on, perhaps indefinitely. So that there may be a consciousness of the events that happened in a whole day or a whole life time. (7.350)

Just as qualities lose their identity when they merge with others to form new qualities, just as feelings generalize to form ideas, and just as ideas generalize to form more general ideas, experiences in short spaces of time are made up of and in turn make up experiences of lesser and greater spaces of time. Consciousness is something that is general and takes up time, as we have said, and though we can only have one consciousness, one idea, at a time, these ideas may be made up of other ideas and processes. For example, I may claim to

be conscious of a particular poem or novel. I have generalized the particular sequence of signs into a title, maybe one
sign. But a poem or novel is not experienced as one sign, at
least initially. A succession of signs make up a literary work
just as a series of instants make up time. It is the continuity
of them that is the medium or mediation of consciousness.

The unlimited complexity of a sign's object and the indefinite continuity of consciousness are but two views of the
same phenomenon, the generalizing tendency. More precisely we might say that the unlimited complexity of the
object that the representamen denotes is the "external," and
the indefinite continuity of consciousness that the interpretant of the sign signifies is the "inward" view of a sign. Because of the generative nature of signs, any change in the
object (such as the addition of the relation-of-the-repre-
sentamen-to-the-object) creates a new interpretant. This is
the basic process by which ideas determine other ideas and is
analogous to the generalizing tendency in qualities and ideas
discussed in earlier chapters. Any number of qualities or
ideas may merge (generalize), but when they do so they lose
their individual identities and become part of the new *quale*-
consciousness or idea. But like qualities, of which in essence
they are generalizations, ideas do not lose their character of
being what they are in themselves. The steamboat smashing
the raft is an idea that is not distinct when we think of the
title *Huckleberry Finn*. But if we have lived through the series
of signs that make up that novel, we have the capacity to
think of any single sign or continuity of signs within the
continuum that is *our experience of Huckleberry Finn*.

Having shown that the very triadic and generative nature of signs makes thought possible, we may now put signs
in Peirce's evolutionary scheme.

For a mind to be capable of logical thought, Peirce says,
it must have three things: "First, ideas; second, determina-

tions of ideas by previous ideas; third, determinations of ideas by previous processes. And nothing will be found that does not come under one of these three heads" (7.348). That is, the mind must have signs of Firstness, Secondness, and Thirdness. In some of the early formulations of his sign theory Peirce designated words, propositions, and arguments as the three things, the three kinds of signs in the mind, necessary for logical thought. Later he found these terms far too limiting and chose other names for the three kinds of interpretants.

How did these arise in Peirce's evolutionary cosmology? What the following will show is that signs we can be conscious of are part of cosmic Thirdness.

We have already defined Firstness, Secondness, and Thirdness as ontological modes of being (possibility, fact, and law) and as experienced in consciousness (feelings, reaction-sensations, and general conceptions). When Peirce analyzed his definition of a sign (as representamen-object-interpretant) in relation to each of these categories, he concluded that a sign or representamen is one of three kinds (Qualisign, Sinsign, or Legisign); it relates to its object in one of three ways (as Icon, Index, or Symbol); and it has an interpretant that *represents* the sign as a sign of possibility, fact, or reason, i.e., as Rheme, Dicent Sign, or Argument. These three sets of three terms are the "trichotomies" in Peirce's semiotic.

The strange words in this paragraph have evoked much confusion and disgust and have been obstacles to the influence of Peirce's thought. But if we keep the following in mind, these terms become quickly understandable: the first term in each trichotomy describes the Firstness of the sign, object, and interpretant; the second term in each trichotomy describes the Secondness of the sign, object, and interpretant; and the third term in each trichotomy describes the Thirdness of a sign, object, and interpretant.

Signs

The following graph shows the relation of the categories and the trichotomies, which is to say the relation of the formal and ontological character of signs. Subsequent discussion will reveal that every embodied sign, i.e., every triadic sign, involves all the formal categories but not necessarily all the material categories of Firstness, Secondness, and Thirdness. Signs signify because of their qualities *and* their relations. The material aspects are predominant in a Qualisign; the relational or formal aspects in a Symbol or an Argument. Literary theorists and linguists who accept a Saussurean, dyadic conception of a sign and focus only on linguistic signs obviously see only the relational-differential character of the sign, but in Peircean theory signs of Thirdness (thought) could not be without signs of Firstness (quality) and Secondness (existent fact) to work upon. Consequently, there is never a complete break between the ontological and phenomenological.

Phenomenological or formal categories		Ontological or material categories		
		Firstness	Secondness	Thirdness
Firstness	A sign is:	a "mere quality" QUALISIGN	an "actual existent" SINSIGN	a "general law" LEGISIGN
Secondness	A sign *relates* to its object in having:	"some character in itself" ICON	"some existential relation to that object" INDEX	"some relation to the interpretant" SYMBOL
Thirdness	A sign's interpretant *represents* it (sign) as a sign of:	"possibility" RHEME	"fact" DICENT SIGN	"reason" ARGUMENT

With this graph before us let us review Peirce's categories and signs. The material aspects of Firstness, Secondness, and Thirdness have been described in previous chapters and are empirically observable. The material aspects of Firstness Peirce called quality, the immediate nonconceptual given of sense experience. The material aspect of Secondness Peirce called "Thisness," the immediate, nonconceptual experience of the dynamic interaction of two things. Existence is dyadic. Ontological Thirdness has much less the character of the immediate given than have the other two categories, but according to Peirce,

> the third category—the category of thought, representation, triadic relation, mediation, genuine thirdness, thirdness as such—is an essential ingredient of reality, yet does not by itself constitute reality, since this category . . . can have no concrete being without action, as a separate object on which to work its government, just as action cannot exist without the immediate being of feeling on which to act. (5.436)

Thus, the material aspect of Thirdness is analogous to time, is the element of continuity.

Formally, or phenomenologically, Peirce holds that "signs may be divided as to their own material nature, as to their relation to their objects, and as to their relations to their interpretants."[3] Peirce held that all thought is reducible to some combination of these three and that this triadic relation is irreducible. He was later to increase the number of formal categories but never revised the concept of a triadic relation of sign–object–interpretant.[4]

Although I will not spell out the comparison, a brief definition of "Qualisign," "Sinsign," and "Legisign" will echo the evolutionary cosmogony given in chapter 1. "A *Qualisign*," according to Peirce, "is a quality which is a sign. It cannot actually act as a sign [be represented] until it is embodied [in a triad of sign–object–interpretant]; but the embodiment has nothing to do with its character as a sign" (2.244). In the beginning was a sign, and that sign was with a quality, and that sign was a quality. All signification came into being through it and without it was no sign made that was made. The only way a Qualisign can be represented is thus:

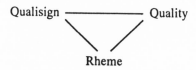

Qualisign ——————— Quality

Rheme

Otherwise, the Qualisign becomes part of the object of another triadic relation, such as:

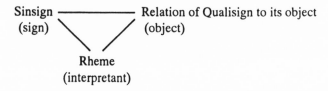

Sinsign ——————— Relation of Qualisign to its object
(sign)   (object)

Rheme
(interpretant)

Now it should be clear why pure Firstness and Secondness, Qualisigns and Sinsigns respectively, are difficult to talk about. They cannot be linguistic signs. No sign can be a word (written or spoken) until it has become a triad of Thirdnesses. A Firstness must undergo three transformations or generations before it can be represented by a word. By now I think the abbreviations for sign, object, and interpretant and for Firstness, Secondness, and Thirdness will be clear.

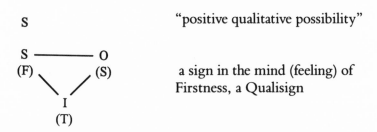

S   "positive qualitative possibility"

S ——————— O
(F)   (S)   a sign in the mind (feeling) of
                                          Firstness, a Qualisign
        I
       (T)

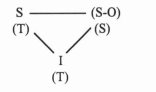
a sign in the mind of a sign in the mind, a Sinsign

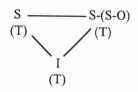
a sign or symbol (possibly a word) in the mind for a sign in the mind of a sign in the mind, a Legisign

If one understands the above, he or she already understands Sinsigns and Legisigns. A Sinsign is a sign that is a fact. Or in Peirce's words, it "is an actual existent thing or event which is a sign" (2.245). The syllable *sin*, Peirce tells us, is taken as meaning "being only once." It can be only once in the sense that it is always and only the second transformation, that is, it is "an actual existent thing or event which is a sign," its object is an embodied Qualisign, and its interpretant is the only Thirdness in the sign. It may be visualized thus:

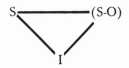

Every Legisign is a sign that represents the relation of a sign in the mind to a sign in the mind. Every thought is a Legisign. Just as the objects of Sinsigns are embodied Qualisigns, the objects of Legisigns are embodied Sinsigns. And just as a Qualisign is a sign that is a quality and a Sinsign "is an actual existent thing or event which is a sign," a Legisign is "a law that is a Sign." "This law is usually established by men. Every conventional sign is a Legisign. . . . It is not a single object, but a general type which, it has been agreed, shall be significant" (2.246). Since it is a general law and not a quality or actual existent object,

> Every legisign signifies through an instance of its application, which may be termed a *Replica* of it. Thus, the word 'the' will usually occur from fifteen to twenty-five times on a page. It is in these occurrences one and the same word, the same Legisign. Each single instance of it is a Replica. (2.246)

But the Replica would not be significant "if it were not for the law which renders it so" (2.246).

A quick reference to Peirce's definitions of Icon, Index and Symbol would reveal that only a Legisign can be a Symbol, i.e., "a sign which would lose the character which renders it a sign if there were no interpretant" (2.304). A Sinsign may be Index or Icon. As Index it is "a sign which would, at once, lose the character which makes it a sign if its object were removed, but would not lose that character if there were no interpretant" (2.304). As Icon it is "a sign which would possess the character which renders it significant, even though its object had no existence" (2.304). Of course a Qualisign can be only an Icon.

Peirce worked out elaborate classifications of the kinds of signs implicit in his theory.[5] A brief look at his ten classes of signs will illustrate two points we have already made. The first is that thought-signs are limited to combinations of signs of Thirdness (i.e., they are all symbolic legisigns). The second is that the three classes of thought-signs, classes eight, nine, and ten on the graph below, correspond to the three things that Peirce said must be in the mind for it to be capable of logical thought: ideas, or words; determination of ideas by previous ideas, or propositions; determinations of ideas by previous processes, or argument.

Charles Peirce's Guess at the Riddle

The following is a bare-bones version of the earlier graph of Peirce's categories and trichotomies overlain with Peirce's ten classes of signs. Note that each line represents one of Peirce's classes of signs, and the numbers indicate the order in which Peirce presents them.

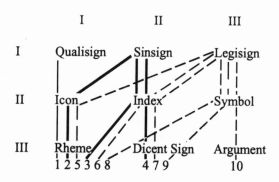

Based upon the fact that Qualisigns and Sinsigns are Firstness and Secondness, respectively, and upon the hypothetical process of sign generation noted above, classes one through four cannot be linguistic signs, that is, they cannot be words or sounds emitted from a person to signify. The interpretant of a Qualisign can be no more than a feeling. A Sinsign is already a combination of signs in that it is always an object of experience (actual existent) that points to another object of experience. Of interest here is the fact that at a more basic level of experience than linguistic signs, we already have *syntax*, a combination that signifies by the nature of the relationship. This is consistent with Peirce's evolutionary theory.

The last six classes involve Legisigns, but classes five, six, and seven are not necessarily linguistic. I take ☺ to be an Iconic Legisign, but I cannot imagine a word that is an Iconic Legisign, except maybe one like "G_ d." Even when they are linguistic signs (e.g., the demonstrative pronoun "that" is a Rhematic Indexical Legisign), they are general laws, habits, conventions that as Icons and Indices picture and point, draw attention to objects other than themselves.

Classes eight, nine, and ten are all Symbols; they draw attention to themselves, to their formal properties, as much as to their referential significance. As I have shown elsewhere,[6] literary art, criticism, and theory are class eight, nine, and ten signs respectively. Peirce changed "Term" to "Rheme" in the third trichotomy, as I mentioned earlier, because "term" was appropriate for only the interpretant of a class eight sign (but not for interpretants of other classes of signs whose interpretant was a Third-Firstness), and because it was inadequate even for a class eight sign. The Rhematic Symbol can be much more complex than "Term" implies because it can embody a virtually unlimited number of objects. It can be a word, sentence, or book (2.292). But for the purposes of the present study it is sufficient to understand that these three classes of signs in Peirce's sign theory correspond to what Peirce in his theory of mind said must be in a mind capable of logical thought: "ideas; . . . determinations of ideas by previous ideas; . . . determinations of ideas by previous processes" (7.348).

BELIEF, REALITY, AND TRUTH

There is nothing . . . to prevent our knowing outward things as they really are, and it is most likely that we do thus know them in numberless cases, although we can never be absolutely certain of doing so in any special case. (5.311)

In the previous chapter we showed some of what is behind Peirce's assertion that for logical thought to be possible, the mind must have three elements: first, ideas, or thoughts; second, general rules according to which one idea determines another, or the habitual connection between thoughts; and third, processes establishing habitual connection between thoughts (7.348, 355, 358). While we have shown that processes can determine ideas, we have not made clear how and to what degree the mind judges and alters its own processes, and thereby the "content" of consciousness.

The "habitual connection between thoughts" is for Peirce synonymous with "beliefs." A belief is not only not present in an instant (as a thought is not present in an instant), "it cannot be present to the mind in any period of time" (7.355). A belief is not the thought of a general rule by which ideas succeed one another, nor is it the succession of ideas; it *is* the rule, "an habitual connection among the things which are successively present" (7.355).

Peirce's treatment of belief in the mind corresponds to

his treatment of "ground" in his sign theory. Therefore we will look first at how ground is treated in Peirce's sign theory and then look at how beliefs can influence and be influenced by thought.

Peirce says "every representamen" is "connected with three things, the ground, the object, and the interpretant" (2.229). This assertion has confused many because "ground" is not quite logically parallel with the "object" and "interpretant." Ground, like belief or the habitual connection of signs, is not a sign itself. Peirce's best single definition of a sign is the following, and it clarifies what he means by ground. Actually, the first sentence is the definition, and the rest is an elaboration of it:

> A sign or *representamen*, is something which stands to somebody for something in some respect or capacity. It addresses somebody, that is creates in the mind of that person an equivalent sign, or perhaps a more developed sign. That sign which it creates I call the *interpretant* of the first sign. The sign stands for something, its *object*. It stands for that object, not in every respect, but in reference to a sort of idea, which I have sometimes called the *ground* of the representamen. (2.228)

All thought, all description, explanation, interpretation of anything is "grounded" in "belief." I have shown elsewhere that Peirce's concept of ground (and hence belief) corresponds to Ludwig Wittgenstein's concept of "language games" and E. D. Hirsch's concept of "genre."[1] The grounds, language games, uses, habitual connections, beliefs are at the basis of all rationality. For a sign even to be thought it must involve a ground. Hence all thought is grounded in habits of thought that are the product of prior volitional acts and social conditioning. We may investigate these habits and alter them, but at no moment can we act or think without the nonrational acceptance of them. This is why Hans-Georg Gadamer says we cannot escape the "horizon" or "historicity" within which we live. This is no doubt why Søren Kierkegaard argues that ultimately all logical and rational systems must begin in a "leap" that is not itself open to rational questioning and inquiry. And this is Wittgenstein's point when he says that questioning must come to an end in order to act.

The processes establishing a habitual connection between thoughts and beliefs Peirce calls "inference." Inference is the process of learning from experience, of doing science. Inference is purposive, deliberate conduct. It involves the comparison of an act, idea, or inference with another and a judgment about future conduct. Future conduct and thought are affected by the beliefs that develop under the influence of a course of self-criticism that inference provides.

A thought, then, is a sign of a belief, of a habitual connection, but is not a belief itself. "A thought which is not capable of affecting belief in any way," Peirce said, "obviously has no signification or intellectual value at all. If it does affect belief it is then translated from one sign to another as the belief is itself interpreted" (7.357). Similarly, an inference translates itself directly into a belief. And a belief that does not determine another thought and ultimately an action ceases to be a belief—a habit of thought. The intellectual character of belief, of habitual connections of ideas, is dependent upon all thought being of the nature of a sign, being capable of endless translation of sign into sign. And here again the psychical and physical meet. Human perceptions and human actions are determined by these habits or beliefs, and they have real consequences. Consequently, we seek beliefs that will "truly guide our actions so as to satisfy our desires," and ones "that we shall *think* to be true" (5.375).

Percept and Percipuum

The relation of thought, belief (habitual connection between thoughts), and inference (process establishing a habitual connection between thoughts and beliefs) in the lived experience of a thinking person is perhaps most clearly treated in Peirce's discussion of the "percept" and the "percipuum."

Just as creation was already in process in any assignable time, "there is no absolutely first cognition of any object, but cognition arises by a continuous process" (5.267). Everything that appears to us, everything that we perceive is the product of mental processes, though we are not aware of them. Our experience is that something, a chair let us say, appears. It obtrudes itself upon us. It makes no profession of any kind, has no intention, does not stand for anything else. It is simply there. It is very forceful in that we cannot deny that it appears. Such is what Peirce calls a "percept" (7.619–24).

Elements of Firstness and Secondness compose any percept. The Firstness of the percept consists of the fact that the quality of feeling or sensation is "something positive and *sui generis*, being such as it is quite regardless of how or what anything else is" (7.625). For example, a particular chair has four legs, a seat, and a back, is yellow, and has a green cushion, but it is singular in that its mode of being is to be one single and undivided whole. Its parts can be separated in thought, but it does not represent itself to have parts. It offers no reason, does not describe itself, and is not subject to belief or disbelief. It simply is (7.625).

Yet these elements are directly perceived as opposed to something else, e.g., as yellow/chair. This is the Secondness, the here-and-now-ness of the percept. A percept is an event that occurs once in an instant. In this sense it is a singular, individual occurrence (7.625).

A perceptual judgment is the apprehension of a percept, that is, the recognition of the character of a percept we think we remember, as when we say "that is a yellow chair." If we *see*, we cannot avoid the percept, and if we "*think* the least thing about the percept, it is the perceptual judgment that tells us what we so 'perceive' " (7.643). The perceptual judgment, e.g., "that appears to be a yellow chair," or "I perceive a yellow chair" professes to represent the percept, which is all that separates it from the percept, which professes nothing. A percept is a single, specific sensation that cannot re-exist; a perceptual judgment is general. "In a perceptual judgment the mind professes to tell the mind's future self what the character of the present percept is. The percept, on the contrary, stands on its own legs and makes no profession of any kind" (7.630). The percept allows its faithful and full interpreter no freedom, but all is prescribed; "the perceptual judgment 'this chair appears yellow' means to say 'take any yellow thing you like, and you will find, on comparing it with this chair, that they agree pretty well in color' " (7.632). Thus the perceptual judgment invites the interpreter to exercise a freedom of choice that the percept precludes (7.632). Because the perceptual judgment represents itself as an index or true symptom of a percept, "we find ourselves impotent to refuse our assent to it in the presence of the percept" (7.628).[2]

In relation to our knowledge and belief a perceptual judgment and percept are much the same. That is, they compel our assent; we cannot go behind them. But whereas the percept contains only two elements, Firstness and Secondness, the perceptual judgment, in that it professes to represent something, is essentially Thirdness, "involves the idea of determining one thing to refer to another" (7.630). Since, as we have established earlier, we can only be consciously aware of (i.e., think about, objectify) Thirdness, we know nothing about the percept except as represented by the perceptual judgment. Peirce treated "the percept as it is immediately interpreted in the perceptual judgment, under the name of the 'percipuum' " (7.643).

A true percipuum and a hallucination, taken in themselves, are no different. If something that others agree to be green appears to me to be red, all that I can say is "I can't help it. That is how I see it" (7.643). The difference between real perception and hallucination is that rational predictions based on the hallucination will likely be falsified. But this is a difference in the way they relate to other perceptions and not a difference in the nature of the perceptions themselves (7.644).

If we wish to understand the nature of human experience, of how humans learn from experience, of how they shape the future, we must consider the percipuum in relation to time. "Experience," Peirce said, "is nothing but the interpretation of the percipua" (7.648). *For us*, the percipuum is the gateway through which the present must pass on the way to the future, but it always evades scrutiny as it passes.

The future, Peirce said, is known only in generalization. The past lacks the explicitness of the present. "[I]n the present moment we are directly aware of the flow of time, or in other words that things can change" (7.643), but time in perception has no ultimate parts or instants. Every part of a lapse of time is a lapse of time (7.651). And "if there is no such thing as an absolute instant, there is nothing *absolutely present*. . . . Thirdness cannot be entirely escaped" (7.653). Even this most basic of all perceptions, the perception of the present moment, involves continuity, or generality, when looked at closely: "its earlier parts being somewhat of the nature of memory, a little vague, and its later parts somewhat of the nature of anticipation, a little generalized" (7.653). Between the "earlier" and "later" parts there must be a central part that is more present, but even that presents the same features as the present moment because time is infinitely divisible, and each part of it is a lapse of time. "[E]very interval of time has a beginning and an end" (7.657). Although the present is continually flowing in upon us, there is nothing absolutely present (7.753). Time is not, on close analysis, composed of instants. Moment melts into moment; succeeding moments are not entirely separate nor yet the same (7.656).

The nature of perception, of the percipuum, as Peirce interpreted it, shows us that nothing in perception is absolutely present and no perception escapes Thirdness. Perception takes place in time, and relates to past, present, and future as time does—that is, is always general. It may be a day, a forenoon, an hour, a minute, a second, and so on, but never an indivisible time or perception. Every percipuum is general, is Thirdness.

Reality and Truth

Having established the nature of the percipuum, we are ready to ask the very important question "whether the testimony of the percipuum is truthful or not" (7.658). To answer this question we must first ask, What is reality? for "There would not be any such thing as truth unless there were something which is as it is independently of how we may think it to be" (7.659). Peirce says that there are three elements of reality. When we speak of "hard facts" we refer to nothing more than the "insistency of the percept, its entirely irrational insistency,—the element of Secondness in it" (7.659). We have already shown that a percept, even a hallucination, cannot be false because it makes no assertion, is not a proposition. But we know nothing about the percept except through the percipuum, and the percipuum has the same insistency and compels acceptance without any assignable reason. In other words, the percipuum is not subject to rational control; we cannot deny what we see. It is only the habits of thought, the beliefs, that are subject to change as a result of logical judgments. The "hard facts," the immediate insistence of percepts upon perceptual judgment, are an important part of reality. We might call it the reality of the present.

A second element of reality is the future, insofar as it is predetermined (7.666). This kind of reality has the compulsiveness that belongs to inductive reasoning, or experimental inquiry. If ideas seem reasonable today, they may seem so to future minds and thereby require certain things to happen in the future. We see this kind of reality dramatized in the fates of tragic heroes and the fulfillment of our expectations. It is the kind of reality that is independent of the thoughts of any particular person "but is not independent of thought *in general*" (7.336). The notion of a reality independent of thought is a contradiction in terms. "What idea can be attached to that of which there is no idea?" Peirce asked (7.345).

The third element of reality is the past, "*something* in it, at least" (7.667). "The future weeds it out [eliminates that which is not real]; but the positive element is peculiar. Memory would be nothing but a dream if it were not that predictions are based on it that get verified" (7.667).

For Peirce, reality is this "threefold force," and the real is "that which the whole process tends . . . to induce our thoughts to rest upon" (7.669). In this threefold process of thoughts determining and causing other thoughts, our experience flows toward a destination, a permanency, a fixed reality that every thought strives to represent. Reality is that toward which the current of thought flows (7.337).

> An idea, a surmise springs up in my mind. It recommends itself to me more or less forcibly as reasonable. . . . That

idea acts upon other ideas and absolutely forces me to say that it requires certain things to happen in the future. The future events come to pass and in part negate my surmise, in part confirm it. (7.669)

The fact that future events negate some representations of perception demonstrates that though we are powerless to deny what appears to us, the percipuum may indeed be false. It could conceivably always contain a false element to be refuted by fresh percipua, which would likewise introduce false elements (7.670). To discover truth, the only method available to a person who cannot deny the insistency of the percipuum but knows it may be false is to repeat the three operations: "conjecture; deductions of predictions from the conjecture; test the predictions by . . . trial" (7.672). Peirce's conception of truth is not something independent of thought. In fact he finds inconceivable a Truth independent of opinions about it. Questions of truth are for Peirce questions of fact, and the essence of truth is its resistance to being ignored (2.136–39). Our experience teaches us that our percipua are remarkably in accord with reality and should be trusted until reality flatly contradicts them.

Peirce's concepts of reality and truth are consistent with his evolutionary cosmology and his theory of triadic, dynamic signs and therefore are future-oriented. Peirce refuses to treat the "real" or "truth" as incognizable or independent of representative relation. It made no sense to Peirce to define the real as "incognizable" because that is to claim knowledge about what is defined as unknowable. Rather he encouraged people "to regard the appearances of sense as only signs of realities. Only, the realities which they represent would . . . be . . . intellectual conceptions which are the last products of the mental action which is set in motion by sensation." The "last products" referred to here are the final and definite opinions "to which the mind of man is, on the whole and in the long run, tending."[3] "The real," Peirce said,

> is that which, sooner or later, information and reasoning would finally result in, and which is therefore independent of the vagaries of me and you. Thus, the very origin of the conception of reality shows that this conception essentially involves the notion of a COMMUNITY, without definite limits, and capable of a definite increase of knowledge. (5.311)

The same goes for truth; "There is . . . to every question a true answer, and final conclusion, to which the opinion of every man is constantly gravitating."[4] Individuals may not live to reach the truth, and general agreement may be postponed indefinitely. This final opinion "is not any particular cognition, in such and such a mind, at such and such a time, although an individual opinion may chance to coincide with it, . . . but is entirely independent of what you, I, or any number or men may think about it." It is "what would be the result of sufficient experience and reasoning" (7.336n).

Our situation is that we never experience objects except through previous signs and are not even conscious of particular signs except as they are denoted in subsequent signs. Therefore, "everything which is present to us is a phenomenal manifestation of ourselves." However, Peirce said, "This does not prevent it being a phenomenon of something without us, just as a rainbow is at once a manifestation both of the sun and the rain" (5.283). Since Peirce saw reality and thought as interdependent rather than incompatible, he could say, "There is nothing . . . to prevent our knowing outward things as they really are, and it is most likely that we do thus know them in numberless cases, although we can never be absolutely certain of doing so in any special case" (5.311).

Thus, the understanding of the percipuum helps us to

see why Peirce held that truth and reality are in the future
and why "we never can be absolutely sure of anything. . . . [P]eople cannot attain absolute certainty con-
cerning questions of fact" (1.147, 1.149). Because reasoning
is the threefold process that can be validated only in the future, and since reality and truth are likewise future-oriented,
they cannot be used as a measure of validity of the particular
judgments and opinions of individuals. About all that we can
determine is whether an argument pursues a method, e.g.,
the threefold method of inductive reasoning, "which, if duly
persisted in, must, in the very nature of things, lead to a
result indefinitely approximating to the truth in the long
run" (2.781).

Thought-signs are dynamic relations, not static objects
or marks on a page. The marks on a page can be nothing
more than representamens (signs in sign/object/interpret-
ant relations). Therefore, inference (all meaning) too is dynamic and takes place in the motion of signs, comes to pass
in the continuity of consciousness. Peirce's theory of signs
in the mind shows us that our individual interpretant "is nothing but another representation to which the torch of truth
is handed along; and *as a representation*, it has its interpretant
again. Lo, another infinite series" (1.339, italics added).

Of course it is one thing to apply logical thought in the
quest for truth about real existent things, Secondness, and it
is quite another to seek "the truth" in relations of pure
Thirdnesses. It is as different as looking to the past and looking to the future. Symbols (signs that are self-consciously
signs of other signs), like qualities, ideas, and the expanding
universe, grow. And possible relations between symbols increase. The character of symbols is to stand in *some* relation
to other symbols. The possibilities of such relations are lim-
itless. To try to fathom what the habit-taking tendency
might evolve in feeling, fact, or thought is like trying to
fathom a black hole in space.

Belief, Reality, and Truth

But if Peirce's theory approximates the truth, several things are reaffirmed. In contrast to the deterministic, nihilistic, absurdist views of human existence that have been dominant for the past one hundred years, Peirce's theory is that creation is working toward logical ends and that individuals are free to participate in that creation process by making the world more and more logical. Goodness that makes a difference in the real world is indeed possible and worthwhile, as the next chapter will show.

5

ESTHETICS, ETHICS, AND LOGIC

Esthetics . . . , although I have terribly neglected it, appears to be possibly the first propedeutic to logic, and the logic of esthetics to be a distinct part of the science of logic that ought not to be omitted. (2.199)

THE PRECEDING CHAPTERS have clarified the human predicament described in the introduction to this book: truth is in the future,[1] but in our consciousness we cannot help but assent to what we perceive to be the case within the particular contexts and language games within which we live. Likewise, at every moment that we perceive beauty and goodness we experience no doubt about what beauty and goodness are. Poststructuralists may conclude from this that beauty, goodness, and truth can be whatever we think they are and that to ask if our perceptions correspond to anything in reality is to be guilty of yearning for a transcendental signified. But Peirce's conceptions of reality and of the nature of signs do not call for the sharp cleavage between the formal and ontological that is found in all theory arising from Ferdinand de Saussure's definition of a sign.[2] In 1903 Peirce bemoaned the "subtle and almost ineradicable narrowness" that runs through "almost all of modern philosophy" that makes the beautiful "relative to human taste," makes "right and wrong concern human conduct only," and thinks "logic deals with human reasoning" (5.128). A purpose, an ultimate end or aim, inherent in the cosmos would give the conceptions of good and bad some basis in reality, would it not? And if there were such an ultimate end, what would be the relationship of the "beautiful" to the "good"? These questions sound very naive in our day and are reminiscent of the efforts of the British moralists of the seventeenth and eighteenth centuries to find a basis for morality in the nature of things. One major difference between Peirce's treatment and that of the British moralists is their radically different perceptions of the "nature of things." Peirce's theory, which rejects the traditional realist and nominalist positions alike, which rejects a mechanistic view of matter as well as a purely formal, indeterminate view of signs, gives new answers to these questions.

After having devoted most of his life to an intensive study of logic, Peirce, in the spring of 1903, in lectures delivered at Cambridge, Massachusetts, under the auspices of the Harvard department of philosophy, told of how he came to recognize the interdependence of esthetics, ethics, and logic.

[W]hen, beginning in 1883, I came to read the works of the great moralists, whose great fertility of thought I found in wonderful contrast to the sterility of the logicians—I was forced to recognize the dependence of Logic upon Ethics; and then took refuge in the idea that there was no science of esthetics, that, because *de gustibus non est disputandum* [about taste there is no disputing], therefore, there is no aesthetic *truth* and *falsity* or generally valid goodness or badness. But I did not remain of this opinion long. I soon came to see that this whole objection rests upon a fundamental misconception. To say that morality, in the last resort, comes to an aesthetic judgment is *not* hedonism—but is directly opposed to hedonism. (5.111)

Charles Peirce's Guess at the Riddle

The goal of this chapter is to elaborate Peirce's reasoning that is suggested in the above quotation, to show why, in Peirce's theory, the concepts of good and bad are essential to any logical thought, and to show what good logic, morals, and esthetics must be in Peircean theory. If indeed Peirce's evolutionary metaphysics can account not only for cosmogony, mind, and logical thought, but also for logical, moral, and aesthetic goodness, it would seem that Peirce had achieved his goal of developing a theory so comprehensive that it can provide a synthesis of all disciplines. While the search for such a synthesis may seem to be a quixotic quest in our time when the strong case for pluralism and relativism has seemingly made outmoded comprehensive architectonic theory, Peirce saw his work merely as the philosophic study of Firstness, Secondness, and Thirdness. The study of these defined for Peirce the three divisions of philosophy: Phenomenology (which treats the "universal Qualities of Phenomena in their immediate phenomenal character"), normative science (which treats the "relation of phenomena to ends"), and metaphysics (which tries "to comprehend the Reality of Phenomena," to treat phenomena in their Thirdness) (5.121–24).

The question of normative science, as Peirce conceived it, is: what are the "universal and necessary laws of the relation of Phenomena to *Ends*"? (5.121). If we remember the role of qualities, reactions, and continuity in Peirce's cosmology, and the role of qualities, ideas, and logical processes in Peirce's theory of mind, we will not be surprised at the role of esthetics, morality, and logic in Peirce's theory of deliberate conduct. Logic studies those things whose end is to represent something; it asks what is true. Ethics considers those things whose ends lie in action; it asks what is good. And esthetics treats those things whose ends are to embody qualities of feeling; it asks what is in and of itself desirable, i.e., beautiful. The essence of these sciences is controlled thought, controlled conduct, and the formulation of habits of feeling.

Peirce's late recognition was that logic is dependent on ethics and ethics on esthetics. If there is to be "control" of action and feeling as well as thought, action and feeling must be, though not dependent on logic for their being, affected by logic. Peirce's fullest treatment of the interdependence of logic, ethics, and esthetics came in the years 1902–1906, some of the last productive years of his life, but the nature of these dependencies is implicit in the cosmology and sign theory to which he had devoted years of study. In the universe, continuity (habit) requires regularity (action) for its being; regularity in turn requires qualities; and quality (*quale*-consciousness) is not dependent on anything else for its being. In signs, every representamen embodies some quality (its being, unity, signifying ability); every representamen is related to a reacting thing (its object); and every representamen determined by another representamen is an interpretant of the latter. Every representamen in thought is a symbol of one of these three characteristics of a sign, that is, is a Rheme, proposition, or Argument. In other words, every thought-sign is a symbol whose interpretant represents it as a sign of quality, fact, or law. It is the capacity of a mind to be aware of and to control its own logical processes that makes normative science, deliberate conduct, possible. An argument, as a representamen, shows separately what *interpretant* it is intended to determine and can be judged by aesthetic, ethical, and logical standards. A proposition, as a representamen, indicates separately in its predicate what *object* it is intended to represent, and can be judged in terms of its quality and veracity. A Rheme represents its representamen in its being as a *sign*, as a simple representation without separate parts, as a sign of possibility that can readily be embodied in a proposition or argument, and cannot be judged by any standard. Consciousness of a sign as Rheme is aes-

Charles Peirce's Guess at the Riddle

thetic experience. Therefore, to introduce the notion of aesthetic goodness or even expressiveness is to introduce comparison, Secondness. For this reason, the role of esthetics in controlled conduct is perhaps the most complex problem for normative science.

The preceding paragraph may take more than one reading to digest, but its major point is that Peirce's treatment of normative science is grounded in his general theory of signs. His aesthetic, ethical, and logical theories are merely the analysis of the possibility of controlled conduct by a consciousness capable of logical thought.

All operations of the mind, Peirce says, may be exactly analogous to inferences except that they are unconscious and therefore uncontrollable and not subject to criticism. But *logic as a normative science is a theory of deliberate thinking*, "logic proper is the *critic* of arguments, the pronouncing them to be good or bad" (5.108). In order for thinking to be deliberate it must be "controlled with a view to making it conform to a purpose or ideal" (1.573). That is, logic involves deliberate approval of one's reasoning. An approval, or any other act, cannot be deliberate unless it is based on a comparison of the thing approved with some ideal or standard. Therefore, it is not possible to reason at all without some general ideal of good reasoning.

Since logic is a kind of deliberate action (self-control in intellectual operations with a view to its conformity to an ideal or standard), it is merely a special case of the theory of controlled conduct. In other words, logic is merely a special case of the theory of the conformity of action to ideals, i.e., ethics, or practics. Most of the time Peirce used the term "ethics" instead of "practics" to refer to the second of the normative sciences. The distinction Peirce made was that "practics" is a theory of *conformity* to ideals; "ethics" is not only a theory of conformity but a theory of *the ideal* itself (1.573). But it is not as if "practics" is amoral. Ultimately, it

makes little difference which term we use, because all reasoning requires self-approval, and self-approval involves
self-control, that is, voluntary acts that our logic approves.
"Now, *the approval of a voluntary act,*" Peirce said, "is a *moral*
approval" (5.130). Since logic is a kind of deliberate action
(self-control in intellectual operations), "the logically good
is simply a particular species of the morally good" (5.130).
Peirce stressed the point repeatedly that logic is the study of
the means of attaining the end of thought and cannot solve
the problem until it knows what the end is (2.198). With an
end in view, it constantly passes judgment on its own processes; right reasoning is reasoning conducive to an ultimate
end (1.611).

> Logical goodness and badness, which we shall find is sim-
> ply the distinction of *Truth* and *Falsity* in general,
> amounts, in the last analysis, to nothing but a particular
> application of the more general distinction of Moral
> Goodness and Badness, or Righteousness and Wicked-
> ness. (5.108)

The "more general distinction" between good and bad
of which logic is a particular application is given to logic by
ethics. "*Ethics,*" Peirce said, "*is the study of what ends of action
we are deliberately prepared to adopt*" (5.130). Ethics is the
normative science *par excellence*, Peirce said, because "an
end—the essential object of normative science—is germane
to a voluntary act in a primary way in which it is germane to
nothing else" (5.130). Right action, righteousness, is action
in conformity to ends we are prepared deliberately to adopt
as ultimate. The business of ethics, in Peirce's view, is not to
designate what is right and what is wrong, but to ask "What
am I prepared deliberately to accept as the statement of what
I am to do, what am I to aim at, what am I after?" (2.198).
Peirce said that we too often confuse an ideal of conduct
with a motive to action. "Every action has a motive; but an

ideal only belongs to a line [of] conduct that is deliberate," to a line of conduct in which "each action, or each important action, is reviewed by the actor and . . . judgment is passed as to whether he wishes his future action to be like that or not. His ideal is the kind of conduct that attracts him upon review" (1.574). There can be no deliberate conduct, no goodness or badness, without an ideal that serves as an aim or standard. Any aim that can be consistently pursued in an indefinitely prolonged course of action becomes, as soon as it is unfalteringly adopted, an ultimate aim. "An aim which *cannot* be adopted and consistently pursued is a bad aim. It cannot properly be called an ultimate aim at all. The only moral evil is not to have an ultimate aim" (5.133).

We will return to the question of what could be an ultimate end or ideal later in the chapter. The question of what the fitness of an ideal consists in is a purely theoretical one for the student of ethics. If we can determine *the ultimate aim*, we know what truly good habits of feeling, good action, and good logic are. Good logic is essentially thought that is under self-control and conducive to our ultimate aim, just as good action is action under self-control and conducive to our purpose. Good esthetics is the deliberate formation of habits of feeling that lead to good actions and good logic. The goodness of habits of feeling, logic, and action is the adaptation of their subjects to their ends.

However, our immediate concern is to examine the process of deliberate control, that is, logic's dependency on ethics and esthetics in our own personal meditations.

How Logic Brings Feelings and Actions under Control

The question is, even if we have an ultimate end, how does logic bring feeling and action under control? If conduct is to be thoroughly deliberate, the review or self-criticism of conduct and the subsequent resolutions about future behavior must determine habits of feeling that will modify future action. If we understand how this modification comes about, we will understand the dependence of logic on esthetics as well as on ethics.

A resolution about future behavior is not a motive for action, but determines a quality of feeling, a passive liking, for a mental formula or way of doing something. And one's own future behavior as well as the actions of others that conform to that way of doing will, on reflection (it is a question whether the feeling felt at any instant is pleasurable), be remembered as having been accompanied by a peculiar quality of feeling, a feeling that is pleasurable. This judgment is what Kant called "aesthetic judgment." Peirce would be in full agreement with Kant that aesthetic judgment is expressive, not cognitive. It is purposive but does not involve conscious purpose. It is not *about* something; it is simply a feeling of judgment we are conscious of as a feeling.

It might be helpful to distinguish between *aesthetic experience* and *aesthetic judgment*. Aesthetic experience is the *feeling* of a quality embodied in an action or object, a feeling that is remembered in a subsequent aesthetic judgment. The feeling and the responsive awareness of it have been determined by previous self-criticisms and resolutions but are at the moment of experience uncontrollable. Hence they are neither good nor bad in themselves. But the aesthetic judgment almost always becomes the object of critical judgment and comparison. That is, it is seen in the context of relationships, which raises questions of fitness, decorum, prudence, effect—in short, goodness and badness. After a way of acting has become habitual, one may no longer consider the aesthetic quality of such a way of doing, but if we stop to ask if our action accords with our earlier resolution, we will be aware, in the very act of finding that our conduct satisfies our resolution, of a feeling of satisfaction that we, directly afterward, recognize as a pleasurable feeling (1.596). *The deliberate development of habits of feeling is the domain of esthetics. Therefore, esthetics is not merely taste, but the forming of taste.*

If we were to focus only on the purely aesthetic (that is, if we focused only on the consciousness of feeling), it would be impossible for there to be a "normative" element in esthetics. If we consider esthetics totally independent of ethics and logic, totally independent of self-criticism and the forming of taste, then there is no such thing as aesthetic goodness or badness, betterness or worseness; there are only various aesthetic qualities. All appearances, objects, and modes of conduct, in and of themselves, may be perceived aesthetically, as having "a multitude of parts so related to one another as to impart a positive simple immediate quality to their totality; and whatever does this is, in so far, aesthetically good, no matter what the particular quality of the total may be" (5.132). In purely aesthetic terms, sweet is not superior to sour, nor are there grades of aesthetic judgment. The terrifying and the beautiful are simply different qualities of feeling. It is the possibility of synthesis in cognitive and practical experiences that makes aesthetic judgments so fundamental to judgments of goodness and truth, though they are in themselves neither good nor true.

The important point here is that for "conduct to be thoroughly deliberate, the ideal must be a habit of feeling (belief) that has grown up under the influence of self-criticism" (1.574). The reason for this is, as we have shown in preceding chapters, that at the moment of experience we are powerless to control our feeling or taste or even our perceptual judgment. Consciously controlled conduct is not something that can happen in an instant, but something that can occur

Esthetics, Ethics, and Logic

over time. All conduct is determined by what has preceded it in time; our critical thought, our judgments and resolutions, our consciously formed habits of feeling determine our future experience and conduct. Our aesthetic judgment, the recognition of pleasure that a particular way of doing brings, follows after the action. It has no real power in itself, but it is the only handle critical thought has on belief and action in the present and future. Thus, esthetics becomes essential for deliberate conduct.

In summary, all deliberate conduct involves (1) some standard or ideal, (2) action, (3) the subsequent comparison of the act with the standard, and (4) judgment about future conduct. Certain kinds of conduct have an aesthetic quality that, when we contemplate them, we think them fine and are led to intend, if we genuinely believe them fine, to make our conduct conform to them. Future conduct is affected by the habits of feeling and thought that grow up under the influence of a course of self-criticism. The process continues. From our judgment that we have a specified belief, we draw certain inferences and conclusions about its efficacy, and the spontaneous development of habits of feeling (belief) is continually going on within us. Thus, deliberate conduct involves critical thinking, ethics, and esthetics.

Peirce's conclusions about the interrelationship of these three "sciences" are the following. "Life can have but one end"; the ultimate must be one; an ideal must be a unity; and ethics defines what that is. "It is, therefore, impossible to be thoroughly rationally logical except upon an ethical basis" (2.198). But what is the ultimate end of action that can be deliberately, reasonably adopted? It must be, Peirce said, "a state of things that *reasonably recommends itself in itself* aside from any ulterior considerations. It must be an *admirable ideal*, having the only kind of goodness that such an ideal *can* have; namely, aesthetic goodness" (5.130). Thus, just as the logically good seems to be a particular species of the morally good, the morally good appears to be a particular species of the aesthetically good.

To Say Morality Comes Down to Aesthetic Judgment Is Not Hedonism

To say that morality, in the final analysis, comes down to an aesthetic judgment seemed to admit hedonism, a conclusion Peirce found shocking. According to this doctrine, Peirce said,

> all the higher modes of consciousness with which we are acquainted in ourselves, such as love and reason, are good only so far as they subserve the lowest of all modes of consciousness. It would be the doctrine that this vast universe of Nature which we contemplate with such awe is good only to produce a certain quality of feeling. (1.614)

The conclusion that morality comes down to an aesthetic judgment seemed to Peirce, at first, to admit hedonism because, he thought, "*gratification, pleasure*, is the only conceivable result that is satisfied with itself." "[S]ince we are seeking for that which is *fine* and *admirable* without any reason beyond itself, *pleasure, bliss*, is the only object which can satisfy the conditions" (1.614). Peirce came to see the fallacy of this argument when he analyzed its two major premises: "first, that it is unthinkable that a man should act for any other motive than pleasure, if his act be deliberate; and second, that action with reference to pleasure leaves no room for any distinction of right and wrong" (1.603).

Peirce's refutation of these premises and of the possibility of pleasure being an ultimate end clarifies the influence of self-criticism on aesthetic experience. In reference to the second premise Peirce asked, "What would be requisite in order to destroy the difference between innocent and guilty conduct?" (1.604). The answer is, of course, that one would have to destroy the ability of self-criticism. As long as one can compare his or her conduct with a preconceived standard, the quality of feeling accompanying any act will be influenced by habits of feeling that have grown up under judgments after similar acts. Aesthetic enjoyment is attending to the total resultant quality of feeling we associate with an object or act we are contemplating. But part of the pleasure is "the sense that here is a Feeling that one can comprehend, a reasonable Feeling" (5.113). This feeling of recognizing the possibilities of meaning, the possibilities of comparison and judgment, is something that can be cultivated and modified over time in response to comparison of one's conduct with a standard. The quality of feeling we discover upon reflection (that is, in aesthetic judgment) to have accompanied an act is not the same as the judgment after the act that the act did or did not satisfy the requirements of a standard; comparisons with a standard and resolutions about future behavior will influence future aesthetic judgments. Therefore aesthetic pleasure or bliss is not merely feeling but an intellectual feeling, a sense that a feeling or consciousness is capable of being represented in thought and subjected to judgment. The hedonist has tried to sever the relation of logical thought to aesthetic judgments. Aesthetic judgment, like all experience, is conditioned by previous acts of consciousness; it is a general feeling.

A close look at the first premise shows it to be a contradiction of the second. What it is "unthinkable" that deliberate action should lack in this premise is determination. So long as determination remains, a person will "pursue a line of conduct upon which he is intent" (1.605), and habits of feeling will be modified by critical judgments. The fallacy in thinking that if morality finally rests on an aesthetic judgment we must admit hedonism, Peirce said, is answered if we see that moral and logical goodness and badness "must begin where control of the processes of cognition begins" (5.114). In other words, moral goodness or badness is not a species of aesthetic approval and disapproval. Moral goodness is action consistent with an ultimate aim. In other words moral goodness is controlled action. It is impossible without critical thought that compares action against a standard. Moral judgment is the evaluation (logical thought, Thirdness) of action (Secondness) according to a standard. But controlled action is still impossible unless there is some way for it to influence feeling and the habits of feeling that guide behavior. If moral and logical judgment makes any difference in behavior, if there is such a thing as deliberate action, it is through the conditioning and evaluation of habits of feeling or beliefs.

The Dependency of Logic and Morality on Aesthetic Judgment

The nature of the dependency of morality on aesthetic judgment is very difficult to state because aesthetic feeling is a consciousness of a sign as "qualitative possibility" that represents "possible objects" in their "characters merely."[3] Aesthetic experience is the perception of signs as not connected with events, actual existents, or acts of reason, but as signs of the immediate, unanalyzable, inexplicable, unintellectual consciousness that "runs in a continuous stream through our lives" (5.289). When one reflects, for example, on a certain action, it has a certain aesthetic quality. He or she may think it fine. Whether the conduct be crude or refined, violent or pacifistic, "a preference between electrocution and decapitation" (1.574), at any particular point in time one's "taste *is* his taste; that is all" (1.591). One's taste will alter in time through the deliberate process of forming habits of belief that we have described earlier, but at any moment what ap-

pears to be aesthetically desirable, what determines a pleasurable quality of feeling, is the possibility that ethics appro-
priates into a judgment of real goodness and badness.

The question of exactly where control begins, at what
point goodness and badness enters, is not easy to pinpoint.
What esthetics offers logical thought are qualities that appear
to us to be fine. To identify a quality of feeling as admirable
is a voluntary act, an ethical judgment. To propose an aesthetic ideal as an ultimate end of action is to move beyond
esthetics. We move, at the moment that critical thought pro-
nounces something fine, from esthetics into ethics and logic.
The moment that a particular fine thing is proposed as an
ideal of action, it is put in relation to Secondness and Thirdness, action and thought. Once an aim has been defined,
conduct can be judged in relation to that, and every judgment, like every other action, will have, on reflection, a
quality of feeling, an aesthetic judgment of approval or disapproval. Esthetics as a part of normative science, as a disci-
pline, is the effort to influence such consciousness of the immediate and of taste by the deliberate formation of habits of
feeling. "If conduct is to be thoroughly deliberate, the ideal
must be a habit of feeling which has grown up under the
influence of a course of self-criticism" (1.574).

Although ethics must begin with aesthetic judgments
and aesthetic judgments are constantly being influenced by
critical thinking, aesthetic judgments have no goodness or
badness, truth or falsity, in and of themselves. Anything
represented in its quality of Firstness, as feeling, is neither
good nor bad (5.158). Even to judge them on the basis of
vividness or expressiveness would be to introduce comparison (5.137). Nonetheless, as the consciousness of the feeling
of thought, aesthetic judgments are foundational to all
thought. They are very like, perhaps a species of, what we
defined earlier as perceptual judgments. The distinction
might be that perceptual judgment is the recognition of the

object of perception; aesthetic judgment is a recognition of the feeling accompanying the perception. Perceptual judgments give reason a perception of "reality"; aesthetic judgments give reason a perception of "value." They are the only handles thought has on truth and goodness at any particular instant. We may reevaluate past judgments, but in active consciousness they are all we have to go on. Aesthetic judgments, then, are not idle activity, merely for those who come and go talking of Michelangelo; they are, Peirce said, judgments of the only respectable kind, ones that bear fruit in the future (1.598).

It is this understanding of esthetics Peirce had in mind when he said that ethics must depend upon esthetics just as logic must depend upon ethics. "Esthetics, therefore, although I have terribly neglected it, appears to be possibly the first propedeutic to logic, and the logic of esthetics to be a distinct part of the science of logic that ought not to be omitted" (2.199).

Once the dependence of thought on feeling is established (every unit of thought—Rheme, proposition, or Argument—has [*is*] a feeling of quality), the dependence of morality on esthetics naturally follows. With the nature of this relation clarified, it no longer seems flippant to say, as Hemingway did, that what is moral is what you feel good after and what is immoral is what you feel bad after. In fact that catches pretty well the dependence of moral goodness on aesthetic judgment. *Feeling good* (pleasure) or *feeling bad* (pain) in one's conscience, *feeling approval or disapproval* after contemplating a painting or text, has no moral or logical goodness, unless we want to declare all these feelings good since they have no fault in them *as feelings*. But such feelings do reflect one's past self-criticism and the habits of feeling formed by the whole community or civilization, and the instant thought recognizes them as a judgment according to some intention or ideal, their goodness or badness becomes real, a description of a real relation, of Secondness. Even if logical thought determines that having a feeling is immoral, the moral goodness or badness is not in the feeling itself or the awareness of the feeling, but in *having it*, that is, in a particular real relation. There is no goodness independent of action, of relations, just as there is no meaning independent of context. Aesthetic experience is the awareness of the possibility of meaning, that is, the awareness of recognizable feelings.

What Can Be the *Ultimate Aim* of Conduct?

Because an ideal must become a habit of feeling if conduct is to be deliberate, it is in the interest of logic and morality that we try to ask of esthetics what would be the ideal feeling. That would surely be the feeling that morality and logic would declare as their ultimate aim. I do not say that we cannot know what that feeling is, but this approach to determining the ultimate aim will not work. It is very difficult, perhaps impossible, to ask of esthetics the question normative science would like to ask it because a standard of comparison is implicit in the question. For example, we may ask, What would we like to experience? As always happens when we talk about Firstness or the immediate moment, we turn the aesthetic experience into something else in the very act of trying to conceive it. To introduce the concept of a goal or an effect is already to move beyond the aesthetic, is already to have incorporated the aesthetic into ethics and logic. The question of esthetics in its purity, Peirce said, must eliminate all consideration of effort, action, and reaction, including all receiving of pleasure, all considerations of self. Even if we ask, What is the one quality that is, in its immediate presence, beautiful?, "beautiful" depends upon the unbeautiful for its mode of being. The word is inadequate. Peirce substitutes the Greek word *kalos*, but that

word is also inadequate, because all words rely on opposi-
tions for meaning. The aesthetic question is, What is desirable in and of itself, for no reason, because of no effect or
comparison? The answer can be nothing other than a quality
of feeling. Any quality of feeling is as good as any other
except in comparison to some standard. Qualities of feeling
are not in themselves either good or bad, but the process of
self-criticism can lead to the deliberate formation of habits
of feeling that can create aesthetic judgments that are judged
to be good in relation to some standard. Even the comparison of an aesthetic judgment to an aesthetic standard, that is,
another aesthetic judgment, is already to have related the aesthetic experience to something else, to have turned a Rheme
into a proposition or an Argument.

The question of what is the ultimate aim of conduct,
which is the only true standard for goodness or badness,
cannot be asked of or answered by esthetics. This brings us
back to ethics. *It is the business of ethics to ask: What end is
possible? What can be an ultimate aim capable of being pursued
in an indefinitely prolonged course of action?* Every ideal is a
general; an ultimate ideal must be a single ideal; it must be a
result that is perfectly self-satisfied but cannot be any sta-
tionary result (1.614). To be ultimate an aim must be immutable under all circumstances and, Peirce said, must "accord
with the free development of the agent's own aesthetic
quality" (5.136).

For Peirce, the only ultimate aim that meets all these
conditions is Reason. Reason "always looks forward to an
endless future and expects endlessly to improve its results"
(1.614). Therefore, as a quality of feeling, Reason is always
satisfied with itself. Reason (not just the human faculty, but
"a something manifesting itself in the mind, in the history
of mind's development, and in nature") is a general that
"never can have been completely embodied."

The very being of the General, of Reason, *consists* in its governing individual events. So, then, the essence of Reason is such that its being never can have been completely perfected. It always must be in a state of incipiency, of growth. . . . [T]he development of Reason requires as a part of it the occurrence of more individual events than ever can occur. It requires, too, all the coloring of all qualities of feeling, including pleasure in its proper place among the rest. (1.615)

The development of Reason, which consists in manifestation, and the creation of the universe are the same. This development is going on today, Peirce said, and will never be done. "I do not see how one can have a more satisfying ideal of the admirable than the development of Reason so understood. The one thing whose admirableness is not due to an ulterior reason is Reason itself" (1.615).

If the development of Reason as Peirce conceived it is the ultimate aim, "the ideal of conduct will be to execute our little function in the operation of the creation by giving a hand toward rendering the world more reasonable whenever . . . it is 'up to us' to do so" (1.615). In other words, the true end of all deliberate conduct (rational thinking and acting) is the survival and extension of rational thought, to make the world more and more rational.

What Kind of Feeling and Conduct Are Called For by Peirce's Ultimate Aim?

Now let us consider, specifically, what conduct and feeling are called for by reason as the ultimate ideal. The general problem of logic, Peirce said, is the problem of probabilities (2.647). Peirce showed that all human affairs (knowledge, predictions, social structures) rest upon probabilities. The real fact that corresponds to the idea of probability is that "a given mode of inference sometimes proves successful and sometimes not, and that in a ratio ultimately fixed" (2.650). In a hundred cases the ratio of successes might fluctuate considerably, but after thousands and millions of cases the fluctuations become less and less and eventually approximate toward a fixed limit. The probability of a mode of argument or inference is "the proportion of cases in which it carries truth with it" (2.650).

Of course any individual inference is either true or false; "in reference to a single case considered in itself, probability can have no meaning" (2.652). Through a series of interesting examples, Peirce showed that "there can be no sense in reasoning in an isolated case, at all" (2.652). For example, suppose that a person's life depends on choosing a red card from one of two packs of cards. One pack contains twenty-five red cards and a black one, and the other pack contains twenty-five black cards and a red one. Peirce said that it would of course be folly not to choose from the pack with the larger proportion of red cards, but what if he drew from the red pack and choose the wrong card?

> [W]hat consolation would he have? He might say that he had acted in accordance with reason, but that would only show that his reason was absolutely worthless. And if he should choose the right card, how could he regard it as anything but a happy accident? He could not say that if he had drawn from the other pack, he might have drawn the wrong one, because an hypothetical proposition such as, "if A, then B," means nothing with reference to a single case. Truth consists in the existence of a real fact corresponding to a true proposition. Corresponding to the proposition, "if A, then B," there may be the fact that *whenever* such an event as A happens such an event as B happens. But in the case supposed, which has no parallel as far as this man is concerned, there would be no real fact whose existence would give any truth to the statement

that, if he had drawn from the other pack, he might have drawn a black one. (2.652)

Probability, then, "belongs to the kind of inference which is repeated indefinitely" (2.652). But this understanding does not obviate the difficulties faced by the person attempting to be rational in his or her behavior. "Although probability will probably manifest its effect in, say, a thousand risks, by a certain proportion between the numbers of successes and failures, yet this . . . is only to say that it certainly will, at length, do so" (2.653). Since humans are finite and the number of risks or probable inferences that they draw in a lifetime are limited, they "cannot be absolutely *certain* that the mean result will accord with the probabilities at all" (2.653). Even taking all their risks collectively, it cannot be certain that they will not fail. Therefore, the case of every person is no different, except in degree, from that of the person drawing a card in the previous example.

Of course the problem faced by individual persons who wish their conduct to be rational is not so much their finiteness as their particularity. "It is an indubitable result of the theory of probabilities," Peirce said,

> that every gambler, if he continues long enough, must ultimately be ruined. . . . If man were immortal he could be perfectly sure of seeing the day when everything in which he had trusted should betray his trust, and, in short, of coming eventually to hopeless misery. He would break down, at last, as every great fortune, and every dynasty, as every civilization does. In place of this we have death. (2.653)

Since we have death, what would happen to all persons will happen to only some persons, but since death makes the number of our risks/inferences finite, it makes their mean result uncertain. Probability and reasoning rest on the assumption that the number of risks/inferences is indefinitely great. Therefore, if we think strictly in terms of our own welfare, reason fails us (2.654).

It is this line of reasoning that led Peirce to conclude that rational behavior requires a social principle that might just as well be called Christian love. He states his opinion thus:

> logicality inexorably requires that our interests shall not be limited. They must not stop at our own fate, but must embrace the whole community. . . . This community, again, must not be limited, but must extend to all races of beings with whom we can come into immediate or mediate intellectual relation. It must reach, however vaguely, beyond this geological epoch, beyond all bounds. He who would not sacrifice his own soul to save the world, is, as it seems to me, illogical in all his inferences, collectively. Logic is rooted in the social principle. (2.654)

To be logical, people must not be selfish, and Peirce gave several examples to show that people are not as selfish as they are often thought to be. "The most popular of all religious tenets," Peirce said, shows "that we can conceive the possibility of a man's descending into hell for the salvation of his fellows" (2.654). Only the inferences of a person capable of heroism and self-sacrifice are really logical. That does not mean that one must be a hero to be logical, but it does mean that one should regard one's own inferences "as being only so far valid as they would be accepted by the hero" (2.654). The person in Peirce's example who had to draw from the two packs, "cannot be logical so long as he is concerned only with his own fate," but such a one can conceive that a person "who should care equally for what was to happen in all possible cases of the sort could act logically." Though he may not be capable of such genuine caring, he can "imitate the effect of that [person's] courage in order to share his logicality" and draw as he would draw. Seen in this way, logicality is attainable whether one is truly capable of selfless heroism or only imitates that virtue. What is required for logical conduct is "a conceived identification of one's interests with those of an unlimited community" (2.654).

In this analysis of logicality, we have come full circle, back to feeling, sentiments. Logicality requires that we care about the entire human community. Peirce said,

> . . . I . . . put forward three sentiments, namely, interest in an indefinite community, recognition of the possibility of this interest being made supreme, and hope in the unlimited continuance of intellectual activity, as indispensable requirements of logic. . . . It interests me to notice that these three sentiments seem to be pretty much the same as the famous trio of Charity, Faith, and Hope, which in the estimation of St. Paul, are the finest and greatest of spiritual gifts. Neither the Old or New Testament is a textbook on the logic of science, but the latter is certainly the highest existing authority in regard to the dispositions of heart which a man ought to have. (2.655)

Thus, reason requires the sentiment of love in order for our conduct to be deliberate. Religion, Peirce said, is "the complete generalization of sentiment" (1.676). We might say that the great religions of the world, particularly Christianity, are precisely the kind of esthetics as normative science that reason as an ultimate aim would require. If the ideal Jesus taught (love: the willingness to sacrifice your own perfection for the perfection of your neighbor) was anticipated by the early Egyptians, the Stoics, the Buddhists, and Confucius, the case is even stronger that love and logicality are two aspects of the same ideal when properly understood. When reason as an ultimate aim becomes a habit of feeling, as it must for conduct to be deliberate, that feeling is love. One cannot act deliberately without both reason and love.

Charles Peirce's Guess at the Riddle

One cannot conform one's conduct to the ideal of reason without the aid of love. However we say it, esthetics, ethics, and logic are all three interdependent and cannot stand alone.

Peirce, in his typical manner, looked at the cosmic consequences of such an ideal, and he discovered the ideal of love to be an evolutionary philosophy, the agapastic theory of evolution he called it, or "evolutionary love" (6.295). "The gospel of Christ says that progress comes from every individual merging his individuality in sympathy with his neighbors" (6.294), and, indeed, according to Peirce, a whole universe has evolved by this very process—the merging of qualities, the generalization of feeling.

6

PHILOSOPHICAL SENTIMENTALISM

If I allow the supremacy of sentiment in human affairs, I do so at the dictation of reason itself; and equally at the dictation of sentiment, in theoretical matters I refuse to allow sentiment any weight whatsoever. (1.634)

IT IS ABUNDANTLY clear that the persons whom Peirce most respected were the true scientists, theoretical reasoners, and metaphysicians. Theory and practice are two masters that such persons cannot serve, for when human desires intervene, the "perfect balance of attention which is requisite for observing the system of things is utterly lost" (1.642). It is "exceedingly desirable, not to say indispensable, . . . for the successful march of discovery in philosophy and in science generally that practical utilities, whether low or high, should be *put out of sight* by the investigator" (1.640). But it is also clear that Peirce thought philosophy, psychology, and most other theoretical disciplines, with the possible exception of mathematics, were in an infantile condition and that most people simply were incapable of careful logical thought. What we might view as the final step in Peirce's theory is his analysis of the role of reason and theory in the conduct of life, in practice. We have touched on this in the previous chapter, where we tried to show that, theoretically, controlled conduct is possible: theory can affect practice. The

83

final candid assessment of Peirce, the logician and pragma-
tist, is that

> in the conduct of life, we have to distinguish everyday
> affairs and great crises. In the great crises, I do not believe
> it is safe to trust to individual reason. In everyday busi-
> ness, reasoning is tolerably successful; but I am inclined to
> think that it is done as well without the aid of theory as
> with it. A *logical utens* [a general idea of what good rea-
> soning is], like the analytical mechanics resident in the bil-
> liard player's nerves, best fulfills familiar uses. (1.623)

Peirce referred to his rationale for this position as his "apol-
ogy for philosophical sentimentalism" (1.632). "Common-
sensism" and "sentimental conservativism" are other labels
he gave this position.

There are, Peirce said, three kinds of reasoning: necessary, which professes only to give information about our
own hypotheses; probability, which is of value only when
we have an endless multitude of insignificant risks; and *il
lume naturale*, an appeal to instinct. In theoretical matters
one may try the suggestions of instinct as hypotheses to be
tested by experience,[1] but beyond that reason gives sentiment no weight. But in practical, human affairs the instincts
and sentiments that have been developed over time by tradi-
tion and custom "are safer guides than one's own feeble ra-
tiocination" because they have been "adapted to the contin-
uance of the race and thus to individual life" (1.661, 7.606).
If one is capable of formal logic, the science of reasoning is
the one theoretical science that may be relied on in dealing
with issues of vital importance. But as we have seen in the
preceding chapter, reason itself "testifies to its own ultimate
subordination to sentiment" and strenuously proclaims the
"supremacy of sentiment in human affairs" (1.672, 1.634).
Therefore, we come back to the first fundamental principle

of sentimental philosophy: the subordination of reason to sentiment.

This view of sentimentalism, Peirce acknowledges, implies conservatism. The exact nature of the conservatism in this case is in "not trusting to one's reasoning powers" in practical matters (1.666). True conservatism does not push any practical principle to an extreme, even the principle of conservatism. As sentimental conservatives, Peirce said,

> We do not say that sentiment is *never* to be influenced by reason [for it is the repeated judgments based on experience over a long period of time by many persons that gives sentiment its authority], nor that under no circumstances would we advocate radical reforms. We only say that the man who would . . . precipitately change his code of morals at the dictate of a philosophy of ethics—who would, let us say, hastily practice incest—is a man whom we should consider *unwise*." (1.633)

The sexual rule against practicing incest is "an instinctive or sentimental induction summarizing the experience of all our race" (1.634). That in itself does not make the rule infallible in any absolute or abstract sense, but it does give the person a "practically infallible" guide, and "he ought to obey it and not his individual reason" (1.633).

It takes very little effort to see that philosophical sentimentalism is a practical version of normative science. Without any theoretical reasoning about esthetics, ethics, or logic, one who gives supremacy to sentiments is capable of moral goodness. Sentimental conservatism and morality are the same thing. Practical morality is "behaving as you were brought up to behave, that is, to think you ought to be punished for not behaving. . . . To be a moral man is to obey the traditional maxims of your community without hesitation or discussion" (1.666). A proposition, maxim, or principle one is willing to act on in great crises is one in which he or she has full belief. Feeling that leads to beliefs (habits of feeling) that enable one to act in accordance with the ideals of one's community can only be judged good. Behavior consistent with such ideals is surely morally good. And the determination to allow sentiment supremacy in practical matters is good logic.

Peirce's tone was sometimes bitter and sarcastic when he was presenting this position, particularly if he was lecturing, because he knew that at the practical level "the only vitally important matter is *my* concern, business, or duty—or yours." Any truly logical person, as defined in the previous chapter, would feel as Peirce did, that as long as this is the case "vitally important facts are of all truths the veriest trifles" (1.672). His scornfulness, then, was directed at the vain self-centeredness of his audience and not at philosophical sentimentalism. Peirce decried the fact that the great attention paid to economic questions during the nineteenth century had "induced an exaggeration of the beneficial effects of greed and of the unfortunate results of sentiment" (6.290). Love, sentimentalism, and public spirit were presented by political economists of Peirce's day as the "source of enduring injury" that should be overruled by prudent self-interests (6.291).[2]

Peirce also distinguished his sentimental conservatism from doctrinaire conservatism that "destroys its own vitality by resisting change and positively insisting, This is eternally right: This is eternally wrong" (2.198). Peirce's philosophical sentimentalism shows how instinct and reason should interact to improve each other. Instincts, sentiments, habits of feeling are our deep and sure substance of soul upon which we depend as we act in the world; "Cognition is only [the soul's] surface, its locus of contact with what is external to it" (1.628). Reason is the "superficial film" of one's being; instinct the "deepest emotional springs" of one's life (1.673). Instinct can grow and develop at a rate "which is slow in the proportion in which it is vital" (1.648). The development of instinct is of the same nature as that of reason (springing from experience) and "takes place through the instrumentality of cognition. The soul's deeper parts can only be reached through its surface" (1.648). Peirce did not denigrate reason, but thought that the process by which the work of theoretical reason penetrates to the core of our being and influences our habits of feeling (and thereby our practical lives) is a slow one, and rightfully so. Sentiments, being influenced by the interaction of reason and feeling over a very long time, are trustworthy in guiding our conduct to beneficial ends.

This view of philosophical sentimentalism may be viewed as Peirce's pragmatic advice about how an individual, without any mathematics or theory of reasoning, can best insure his or her own survival, success, and prudent behavior. But for philosophical sentimentalism to be a guide to truly moral and logical goodness, the sentiments on which we rely cannot be selfish, but must be "a generalized conception of duty which completes [our] personality by melting it into the neighboring part of the universal cosmos" (1.673). Peirce consistently held that the mental qualities we most admire are not logical finesse but devotion, courage, loyalty, and modesty. Such qualities give evidence that a person's sentiments have been generalized beyond self-interests. These are the sentiments that make society possible.

No wonder Peirce came to a new appreciation of poetry and ethics. "Poetry," he says,

> is one sort of generalization of sentiment, and in so far is the regenerative metamorphosis of sentiment. But poetry remains on one side ungeneralized, and to that is due its emptiness. The complete generalization of sentiment is religion, which is poetry, but completed poetry. (1.676)

The religion Peirce referred to in the above quotation is the Christian faith understood as belief in the law of love, a belief that has the earmark of truth because it was anticipated from the primitive ages by ancient Egyptians, Stoics, Buddhists, and Confucius. Peirce said that a little exclusive church that walls people out with its creeds and doctrinal touchstones is a narrow and sordid affair. "Man's highest developments are social," he said, "and religion . . . only comes to full flower in a great church coextensive with a civilization. . . . A great catholic church is wanted" (6.442–43).

Conclusion

This book began with an account of the tendency of qualities to merge, to generalize. We traced the development of generalization of feeling as it gave birth to cosmos and ideas and logical thought. Next, we asked of reason, At what should we aim? How should we act? And the answer to those questions that we are now able to receive finds its echo in each of the foregoing chapters. The answer has two parts, one from reason and one from sentiment, and is Peirce's credo for philosophical sentimentalism.

> [R]easoning and the science of reasoning strenuously proclaim the subordination of reasoning to sentiment.
>
> . . .
>
> [T]he very supreme commandment of sentiment is that man should generalize . . . , should become welded into the universal continuum. (1.673)

In Peircean theory, the generalization of feeling has given birth to a cosmos of regularities and ideas. Each feeling, each idea, each person has a quality of feeling when considered in itself, but is capable of further generalization. To

Philosophical Sentimentalism

generalize one's sentiments, one's self, one's interests, is to participate in making the world more logical, to participate in the agapastic evolution of the creative consciousness of the universe.

Peirce's "guess at the riddle" offers a theory and its practical application in human affairs that the world could "live" with, literally.

NOTES

Preface

1. I borrow this term from Marike Finlay, *The Potential of Modern Discourse: Musil, Peirce, and Perturbation* (Bloomington: Indiana University Press, 1990).

2. Douglas Hofstadter, *Gödel, Escher, Bach: An Eternal Golden Braid* (New York: Vintage Books, 1979), pp. 103–26.

3. *The Chronicle of Higher Education*, 4 May 1988: B1–2. The article is about Hawking's *A Brief History of Time: From the Big Bang to Black Holes* (New York: Bantam Books, 1988).

4. This phrase is from Michael Raposa's *Peirce's Philosophy of Religion* (Bloomington: Indiana University Press, 1989), p. 6. Vincent G. Potter, S.J., in his book *Charles S. Peirce on Norms and Ideals* (Amherst: University of Massachusetts Press, 1967), pp. ix–x, briefly reviews the earlier positions of scholars about whether or not Peirce outlined a "genuine philosophical 'system'" or left a "patchwork of incompatible tendencies."

5. *The Collected Papers of Charles Sanders Peirce*, vols. 1–6, ed. Charles Hartshorne and Paul Weiss, 1931–1935; vols. 7–8, ed. A. W. Burks, 1958 (Cambridge, Mass.: Harvard University Press), 1:354n. *The Collected Papers* dates this work c. 1890. However, according to Nathan Houser, the Peirce Project has determined that 1886 is a more accurate date. Future references to *The Collected Papers* are parenthesized within the text. The first numeral in the reference is the volume number, and the number to the right of the point is the paragraph.

6. On at least two occasions, in 1895 and 1907, Peirce quoted from Emerson's poem "The Sphinx," in which the Sphinx asks:

"Who'll tell me my secret,
   The ages have kept?—

. . . .
The fate of the man-child;
   The meaning of man[?]"

7. *Writings of Charles S. Peirce: A Chronological Edition*, ed. M. Fisch et al., four volumes now completed (Bloomington: Indiana University Press, 1982-), p. xi.

8. *The Collected Papers* dates this draft c. 1898. I rely here on Nathan Houser and the Peirce Project for what seems to be a more accurate date.

1. Peirce's Cosmogonic Philosophy

1. See Michael L. Raposa, *Peirce's Philosophy of Religion* (Bloomington: Indiana University Press, 1992), for an extensive treatment of Peirce's religious ideas.

2. This concept is more fully developed in the final chapter.

3. "Chance" is not arbitrariness of dead matter. Rather it is a characteristic of Firstness. Firstness is vital, sentient, and the force behind evolution. "Thus, when I speak of chance," Peirce says, "I only employ a mathematical term to express with accuracy the characteristics of freedom or spontaneity" (6.201).

4. In the analysis that follows, it is "feeling," what Peirce describes as "*quale*-consciousness," that is the "other element" that cannot be accounted for except metaphysically.

5. For a comprehensive treatment of Peirce's conception of God, see Michael L. Raposa's *Peirce's Philosophy of Religion*. His treatment of God as Nothingness is on pages 70–71.

6. Peirce goes to some length to explain his doctrine of objective chance, or "tychism," which is a fundamental ingredient in his cosmology. The fortuitous variation, chance spontaneity, or deviation from regularity is integral to Peirce's cosmological evolutionary theory. As will be explained in the subsequent pages, the principle of habit, which underlies all law and order in the universe, was "itself due to the growth by habit of an infinitesimal chance tendency toward habit-taking" (6.262).

7. To understand Peirce's notion of *quale*-consciousness, of sentiency, one must not think of physical entities, atoms for example, with sentiency superadded to them. That, Peirce granted, "would be feeble enough. But what I mean is, that *all that there is*, is First, Feelings; Second, Efforts; Third, Habits—all of which are more familiar to us on their psychical side than on their physical side; and that dead matter would be merely the final result of the complete induration of habit reducing the free play of feeling and the brute irrationality of effort to complete death. Now I would suppose that that result of evolution is not quite complete even in our beakers and crucibles" (6.201, italics added).

8. Peirce's doctrine of continuity (generality, law, regularity), he called synechism. Thus, tychism and synechism are opposing prin-

ciples, yet tychism gives birth to new uniformities and synechism is never entirely free of chance.

9. This graphic illustration is in the text of *The Collected Papers of Charles Sanders Peirce*, 6.206.

10. An excellent study of how these categories evolved in Peirce's thought is Joseph L. Esposito, *Evolutionary Metaphysics: The Development of Peirce's Theory of Categories* (Athens: Ohio University Press, 1980).

2. Mind

1. *Evolutionary Metaphysics: The Development of Peirce's Theory of Categories* (Athens: Ohio University Press, 1980), p. 56.

2. For further treatment of divine transcendence and immanence see Raposa's *Peirce's Philosophy of Religion*, pp. 50–52. Raposa agrees with those who say "Peirce . . . , while definitely not a pantheist, might be properly labeled a *panentheist*, that is, one who views the world as being included in but not exhaustive of the divine reality" (p. 51).

3. See particularly 5.313–14, 6.270–71, and 7.583–90 for Peirce's comparison of a person with an idea or word.

4. In the early 1890s Peirce wrote, "This theory has been ridiculed by theologians as the merest whimsey while philosophers have pronounced it absurd upon metaphysical grounds; but students of physical and natural science are somewhat more favorable to it. Its advocates maintain that it is a perfectly consistent and legitimate working hypothesis, that it unmistakably commits itself to certain predictions and predesignations, that its truth or falsity ought to be judged exclusively from the comparison of these consequences of it with observation, and that, as far as it has been carried, this comparison has been quite favorable to the theory" (6.277).

5. Even though it is a truism that Peirce's writings are difficult to read, Peirce was a good stylist. I quote extensively from Peirce in the next few paragraphs because of the clarity and effectiveness of his descriptions. Peirce's examples, figurative language, and extended analogies help us to understand and remember his concepts.

3. Signs

1. This sentence is accurate, but it might be clearer if it were more redundant, as follows: Our only experience of Firstness and Secondness *that we can know anything about, be aware of, remember, or learn from* is mediated by Thirdness.

2. Parts of this chapter have previously been published in *The Fate of Meaning: Charles Peirce, Structuralism, and Literature* (Princeton, N.J.: Princeton University Press, 1989).

3. 12 October 1904, *Charles S. Peirce's Letters to Lady Welby*, ed. Irwin C. Lieb (New Haven, Conn.: Whitlock's, 1953), p. 12.

4. For more on Peirce's further classification of signs, see Peirce's letter of 23 December 1908 to Lady Welby in *Semiotic and Significs: The Correspondence between Charles S. Peirce and Victoria Lady Welby*, ed. Charles S. Hardwick (Bloomington: Indiana University Press, 1977), pp. 73–86; "Irwin C. Lieb on Peirce's Classification of Signs," which is Appendix B in Hardwick's *Semiotics and Significs*, pp. 160–66, and first appeared in *Letters to Lady Welby*; and Gary Sanders, "Peirce's Sixty-Six Signs?" *Transactions of the Charles S. Peirce Society*, vol. 6, no. 1 (Winter 1970), pp. 3–16.

5. I recommend David Savan's *An Introduction to C. S. Peirce's Full System of Semeiotic* (Toronto: Toronto Semiotic Circle, 1987) to readers who wish to study Peirce's classification of signs in more detail.

6. I refer here to my book *The Fate of Meaning: Charles Peirce, Structuralism, and Literature* (Princeton, N.J.: Princeton University Press, 1989), which is still the most extensive application of Peirce's semiotic to literary art, criticism, and theory.

4. Belief, Reality, and Truth

1. *The Fate of Meaning: Charles Peirce, Structuralism, and Literature* (Princeton, N.J.: Princeton University Press, 1989), pp. 94–98.

2. E. D. Hirsch's treatment of "meaning" and "interpretation" in *Validity in Interpretation* (New Haven, Conn.: Yale University Press, 1967) is very similar to Peirce's treatment of "percept" and "perceptual judgment." "Significance" for Hirsch would be an additional step away from the "percept" or "meaning."

3. "Critical Review of Berkeley's Idealism," *Charles S. Peirce: Selected Writings (Values in a Universe of Chance)*, ed. Philip P. Weiner (New York: Dover, 1958), pp. 83, 82.

4. Ibid., p. 81.

5. Esthetics, Ethics, and Logic

1. From the individual human perspective, truth is in the future in the sense that it is the final settled opinion that would result from

sufficient experience and reasoning by a human community without limits. Possibly, an individual's opinion might coincide with the final settled opinion, but there is no way to know or recognize when or if that happens (7.336n).

2. See John Sheriff, *The Fate of Meaning: Charles Peirce, Structuralism, and Literature* (Princeton, N.J.: Princeton University Press, 1989), for an overview and critique of contemporary literary theory and an argument for Peircean theory as an alternative.

3. 23 December 1908, *Charles S. Peirce's Letters to Lady Welby*, ed. Irwin C. Lieb (New Haven, Conn.: Whitlock's, 1953), p. 31.

6. Philosophical Sentimentalism

1. Peirce's treatment of abduction argued that there is a tendency to "guess right" in making scientific hypotheses. Since laws of matter and of mind are the same, it is reasonable that "there may be some natural tendency toward an agreement between the ideas which suggest themselves to the human mind and those which are concerned in the laws of nature" (1.81).

2. Peirce quoted the words in quotation marks from Simon Newcomb's *Principles of Political Economy* (New York: Harper and Brothers, 1886). It was, Peirce said, "the most typical and middling [handbook of political economy] I have at hand" (6.291).

INDEX

John K. Sheriff is E. E. Leisy Professor of English at Bethel College. He is the author of *The Fate of Meaning: Charles Peirce, Structuralism, and Literature*; *The Good-Natured Man: The Evolution of a Moral Ideal, 1660–1800*; and articles on semiotics and literary theory.